ABC, Follow Me!
Phonics Rhymes and Crafts, Grades K-1

Linda Armstrong

LINWORTH LEARNING

Activities & Resources From the Minds of Teachers

Published by Linworth Publishing, Inc.
3650 Olentangy River Road, Suite 250
Columbus, OH 43214

Copyright © Linworth Publishing, Inc., 2007

The purchaser is entitled to reproduce all patterns for use in an individual classroom or library. Any other use or reproduction requires written permission from the publisher.

1-58683-230-1

5 4 3 2 1

Table of Contents

Table of Figures vi
About the Author viii
Acknowledgements viii
Introduction ix
Art Project List xiii
Standards Correlation Chart xiv

SECTION 1: The Alphabet: Symbols and Sequence 1
Introduction 1
   Unit 1: Alphabet Symbols 5
      ABC, Follow me! A verse introducing each letter with a sample word 5
      Y is for You and M is for Me: An Initial Crown:
         A crown using the child's initial 7
      An Initial Crown Pattern: A work page with take-home suggestions 8
      Two Side Headbands for the Crown with Upper and Lower Case Letters 9
   Unit 2: Upper Case and Lower Case Letters 10
      Upper Case and Lower Case: A Shape-shifting Verse 10
      Upper Case, Lower Case, Our Names are the Same! 11
      Lower Case Cards: Cards to be used with the verse 12
      Upper Case Cards 13
      Magic Letters: A craft project. Letter rubbings with pencil or crayon 14
      Upper and Lower Case Hh Pattern: A work page with take-home suggestions 15
   Unit 3: Alphabet Sequence 16
      Putting the Alphabet in Order: A verse teaching alphabet sequence 16
      Before, After, Between 16
      Alphabet Chains: Paper chains with an alphabetical order twist 17
      Alphabet Chain Pattern Page 18

SECTION 2: Consonants 19
Introduction 19
   Unit 1: M 21
      M is for Moth: A verse teaching the sound of M 21
      M is for Mask Art Project: A mask based on the letter M 23
      M is for Mask Pattern: A reproducible pattern page 24
      Cartoon Animal Eyes, Noses, and Ears for the M Mask: A reproducible
         source of components usable for several projects 25
   Unit 1: S 26
      S is for Sun 26
      S is for Sun: A verse that teaches the sound of the letter S 26
      Sun Symbols: A coloring page that invites originality 27
      Sun Symbol Pattern: A reproducible pattern page 28

Table of Contents CONTINUED

Unit 3: T 29
- **T is for True** 29
- *Is it Tricky or is it True?* A verse that teaches the sound of the letter T 29
- **Truly Tricky Ties:** A paper necktie based on the letter T 30
- **T is for Tie pattern:** A reproducible pattern page 31

Unit 4: H 32
- **H is for Hand:** A verse that teaches the sound of the letter H 32
- *Can You Hold it in Your Hand?* 32
- **Dream Hands:** A simple tracing project that encourages abstract thinking 33

Unit 5: K 34
- **Key to K Kingdom** 34
- *K is for Key:* A verse that teaches the sound of the letter K 35
- **K is for Key: Flannel Board Patterns or a Coloring Page:** Illustrations for the rhyme or a coloring page 36
- **K is for Key: Clay Impressions:** Directions for a key impression in craft dough 37

Unit 6: B 38
- **B is for Book** 38
- *B is for Book:* A verse that teaches the sound of the letter B 39
- **A B Book:** Directions for a center-folded book 40
- **A B Book Pattern:** A small book pattern. (If child-authored book pages are cut to this size, the center may be stapled with a regular, rather than a long-necked, stapler.) 41

Unit 7: F 42
- **F is for Fun!** 42
- *Would it be Boring, or Would it be Fun?* A rhyme to teach critical thinking, as well as the sound of F 43
- **F is for Funny Face:** A paper plate clown face 44

Unit 8: L 45
- **Lanterns, Leopards, and Launches** 45
- *L is for Light:* A verse to teach the sound of the letter L 45
- **L is for Lantern:** A cut paper lantern 46
- **Paper Lantern Pattern:** A reproducible pattern page 47

Unit 9: N 48
- **Nodding for N** 48
- *N is for Nature:* A verse that teaches the sound of the letter N 49
- **N is for Nature:** A traced leaf project 50

Unit 10: D 51
- **Danny and Darla: D Detectives** 51
- *D is for Detective:* A verse that teaches the sound of the letter D 52
- **D is for Dino-rama:** A dinosaur diorama to color, cut, and paste 53
- **A Dino-rama Pattern:** A reproducible pattern page 54

Table of Contents CONTINUED

Unit 11: W 55
- **What Goes in the Wagon?** A verse that teaches the sound of the letter W 55
- **W is for Weaving:** A paper weaving project 57
- **Pattern for Paper Weaving Warp:** A paper "loom." 58
- **Pattern for Paper Weaving Weft:** Weaving strips 59

Unit 12: C 60
- **C is for Color** 60
- **C is for Color:** A verse that teaches the sound of the letter C 60
- **C is for Color Wheel:** A project that teaches color families 61
- **Color Wheel Pattern:** A reproducible pattern page 62

Unit 13: G 63
- **Goggles** 63
- **G is for Goggles:** A skin-diving verse that teaches the sound of the letter G 64
- **A Goofy Goggles Craft:** Instructions for creating paper goggles 65
- **A Goggles Pattern Page:** A reproducible pattern page 66

Unit 14: J 67
- **Jewels** 67
- **J is for Jewelry:** A verse about costume jewelry that teaches
  the sound of the letter J 67
- **J is for Jewelry:** Directions for a paper jewelry project 68
- **Patterns for J Bracelets:** A reproducible pattern page for paper bracelets 69

Unit 15: R 70
- **Rattle, Roar, and Rumble** 70
- **R is for Rattle:** A verse that teaches the sound of the letter R 71
- **R is for Rattle: A Water Bottle Rattle:** Dried beans in a water bottle
  make a great sound! 72
- **A Label for a Water Bottle Rattle:** A reproducible pattern 73

Unit 16: P 74
- **People, People, People** 74
- **P is for People:** A verse that teaches the sound of the letter P 74
- **Folded Paper People:** Paper people in a string 75
- **Pattern for Paper People:** A reproducible pattern..76

Unit 17: V 77
- **V is for Vegetable** 77
- **In a Very Green Valley:** A nutritious verse that teaches the sound of the letter V 78
- **Flannel Board Patterns for V is for Vegetables:** A reproducible pattern page......79
- **V is for Vegetable Print:** Instructions for making prints with cut carrots 80

Unit 18: Y 81
- **Yell, Yell, Yellow** 81
- **Y Riddles** 81
- **Yell, Yell, Yellow!** A verse that teaches the sound of the letter Y 82
- **Y is for Yellow Leaves:** A Sponge Print Project 83
- **Letter Y: A Tree Trunk Pattern:** A reproducible coloring page 84

Table of Contents CONTINUED

    Unit 19: Z 85
        Zoom, Zing, Zone, Zap! 85
        Z Words 85
        Zoom, Zing, Zone, Zap! A verse that teaches the sound of the letter Z 86
        Z is for Zigzag: An Accordion Book 87
        Pattern for a Letter Z Accordion Book: A blank accordion book
            with take-home suggestions 88
    Unit 20: Q 89
        Q is for Quilt, Quiet, and Quick 89
        Q is for Quilt: A verse that teaches the sound of the letter Q 89
        Q is for Quilt: A Quilt Square Project: Directions for
            two classic quilt squares 90
        Pattern for Two Quilt Squares: A coloring page with take-home suggestions......91
    Unit 21: X 92
        X is the End of Box 92
        B-O-X Spells Box: A verse that teaches the sound of the letter X 92
        X Ending Cards: Cards to accompany the verse 93
        Glowing X's: A Wax Resist Project: X's stand out against a black background......94
    Unit 22: Medial Consonants 95
        Middle Riddles 95
        Hinky Pinkies: A set of "hinky pinky" medial consonant riddles....................95
        Funny Bunny: Directions for a very hoppy cut-and-color project 96
        Funny Bunny Pattern: A reproducible pattern page 97

Section 3: Vowels 99

  Introduction 99
  Unit 1: Alphabet Symbols 101
        Nat, Net, Not, Nut! Hooray for Short Vowels! (C-V-C)...........................101
        Nat, Net, Not, Nut! A verse that contrasts the sounds of all five short vowels 102
        Word Bugs Project: A cut-and-color paper sculpture project....................103
        A Lady Bug Pattern: A reproducible pattern page 104
  Unit 2: Short A 105
        A Flat Bat and Other Short A's 105
        Cat, Hat, Pan, Bat: A verse that teaches the sound of short A...........................105
        A Flat Bat Craft Project: Directions for a batty cut-and-color project 106
        Flat Bat Pattern: A reproducible pattern page...107
  Unit 3: Short E...108
        Red Leg Web Neb: A Nonsense Verse 108
        Red, Leg, Web, Neb: A nonsense verse...108
        Magic Red: A Red and Green Vibrating Target: A complementary
            color project 109
        Magic Red Pattern: A reproducible pattern page 110

Table of Contents CONTINUED

Unit 4: Short I 111
    Inkso, Blinkso, I Don't Think So! A verse that teaches the sound of short I. ..111
    Something Fishy: A Mobile 112
    Fish Patterns for the Mobile or for Coloring: A reproducible pattern page 113

Unit 5: Short O 114
    The Blob: Short O 114
    The Blob: A verse that teaches the sound of short O 115
    The Blob: An Art Project: A coloring activity that encourages creativity 116
    The Blob Pattern: A reproducible pattern page 117

Unit 6: Short U 118
    Where is the Bus? A verse that teaches the sound of short U 118
    Cut it Out! A fold and cut paper project 119
    Paper Lace Pattern: A reproducible pattern page 120

Unit 7: Long Vowels 121
    The Vowel Says its Name 121
    The Long and Short of It: A rhyme introducing long vowel sounds 121
    A Note Card: A Long Vowel Art Project: An instruction page 122
    A Note Card Pattern: A pattern for a note card 123

Unit 8: Long A 124
    Long A, as in Snake: A Cumulative Rhyme 124
    Dake, Hake, Nake-ee-Oh!: Phrases are added with each verse
        of this long A verse 124
    Snakes! Directions for a paper snake project, with a craft clay recipe
        and craft recipe websites 125
    Paper Snake Pattern Page: A reproducible pattern page 126

Unit 9: Long I 127
    Let's Take a Hike! A long I response verse based on "The Lion Hunt." 127
    Kite Bookmarks: Take flight with these bookmarks 129
    A Kite Pattern: A reproducible pattern page 130

Unit 10: Long O 131
    Homes: A Long O Verse 131
    This Home, That Home: A verse that is right at home with long O's 131
    A Drawing of Home: Directions for a drawing activity 132
    Long O Riddles 132

Unit 11: Long U 133
    What's Missing? A Rhyme: A long U verse 133
    Long U is in Blue: A torn paper art activity 134

Appendix 135
Word Lists for Exercises, Verses, and Practice Cards 135
    Initial Consonant Words 135
    Medial Consonant Examples 136
    Short Vowels in Consonant-Vowel-Consonant Words 136
    Long Vowels in Consonant-Vowel-Consonant-E Words 136

Selected Resources 137

Table of Figures

SECTION 1: The Alphabet: Symbols and Sequence 1
    Figure 1.1 A Crown Photograph 7
    Figure 1.2 A Crown Pattern 8
    Figure 1.3 Two Strips with Letters 9
    Figure 1.4 Lower Case Cards 12
    Figure 1.5 Upper Case Cards 13
    Figure 1.6 An Hh Rubbing Scan 14
    Figure 1.7 An Hh Rubbing Pattern 15
    Figure 1.8 A Photograph of an Alphabet Chain 17
    Figure 1.9 Alphabet Strip Patterns 18

SECTION 2: Consonants 19
    Figure 2.1 A Picture of a Finished Mask 23
    Figure 2.2 A Pattern for a Large Outline M 24
    Figure 2.3 Cartoon Animal Eyes and Noses 25
    Figure 2.4 A Scan of a Finished Sun Symbol 27
    Figure 2.5 A Sun Symbol Pattern 28
    Figure 2.6 A Scanned Finished Necktie 30
    Figure 2.7 A Necktie Pattern 31
    Figure 2.8 A Scanned Sample of Hand Art 33
    Figure 2.9 K Flannel Board Patterns or a Coloring Page 36
    Figure 2.10 A Photograph of a Finished Key Impression 37
    Figure 2.11 A Photograph of a Finished B Book 40
    Figure 2.12 A B Book Pattern 41
    Figure 2.13 A Picture of a Finished Funny Face 44
    Figure 2.14 A Photograph of a Finished Lantern 46
    Figure 2.15 A Lantern Pattern 47
    Figure 2.16 A Sample of Traced Nature 50
    Figure 2.17 A Sample of a Dinosaur Diorama 53
    Figure 2.18 A Dino-rama Pattern 54
    Figure 2.19 A Photograph of a Finished Paper Weaving Project 57
    Figure 2.20 A Pattern for Paper Weaving Warp 58
    Figure 2.21 A Pattern for the Paper Weaving Weft 59
    Figure 2.22 A Pattern for a Color Wheel 62
    Figure 2.23 A Photograph of the Finished Goggles Project 65
    Figure 2.24 A Goggles Pattern 66
    Figure 2.25 A Photograph of Finished Paper Bracelets 68
    Figure 2.26 Patterns for J Bracelets 69
    Figure 2.27 Photograph of a Water Bottle Rattle 72
    Figure 2.28 A Label for a Water Bottle Rattle 73
    Figure 2.29 A Pattern for Folded Paper People 76
    Figure 2.30 Vegetable Flannel Board Patterns 79
    Figure 2.31 A Photograph of a Sample Vegetable Print Card 80
    Figure 2.32 A Scan of a Sponge-printed Leaf 83
    Figure 2.33 A Scan of a Finished Letter Y Tree Picture 83
    Figure 2.34 A Letter Y Tree Trunk Pattern 84

Table of Figures CONTINUED

Figure 2.35 A Photograph of a Finished Zigzag Book 87
Figure 2.36 A Pattern for an Accordion Book 88
Figure 2.37 A Scan of the Finished Quilt Squares 90
Figure 2.38 A Pattern for Two Quilt Squares 91
Figure 2.39 Cards for Words Ending with X 93
Figure 2.40 A Scan of a Wax Resist Project 94
Figure 2.41 A Photograph of Funny Bunny 96
Figure 2.42 A Pattern for Funny Bunny 97

SECTION 3: Vowels 99

Figure 3.1 A Photograph of the Finished Ladybug..................................103
Figure 3.2 A Ladybug Pattern 104
Figure 3.3 A Photograph of a Finished Bat 106
Figure 3.4 A Flat Bat Pattern 107
Figure 3.5 A Scan of a Finished Red and Green Target 109
Figure 3.6 A Red and Green Target Pattern 110
Figure 3.7 A Photograph of a Finished Fish Mobile 112
Figure 3.8 Fish Patterns for the Mobile or for Coloring..........................113
Figure 3.9 A Scan of a Finished Blob Drawing 116
Figure 3.10 A Blob Pattern 117
Figure 3.11 A Scan of Finished Paper Lace 119
Figure 3.12 A Paper Lace Pattern 120
Figure 3.13 A Scan of a Finished Note Card 122
Figure 3.14 Note Card Pattern 123
Figure 3.15 A Photograph of a Finished Spiral Snake 125
Figure 3.16 A Paper Snake Pattern 126
Figure 3.17 A Scan of a Finished Kite Bookmark 129
Figure 3.18 A Pattern for a Kite Bookmark 130
Figure 3.19 A Scan of a Sample House Drawing....................................132
Figure 3.20 A Scan of a Sample Torn Paper Cloud Picture 134

About the Author

Before moving to Colorado, Linda Armstrong was an educator in Los Angeles. She served first as a classroom teacher, and later as a Language Development Resource Teacher based in the school library. She told stories in costume, presented puppet shows, sponsored a drama club, and coordinated a school-wide Language Arts festival.

Now, Linda writes books for children and their teachers. Her credits include more than twenty adaptations of classic stories, a collection of contemporary free verse, a middle grade novel, a book of art projects for elementary teachers, and several phonics books. She has also written supplementary classroom materials for history, reading comprehension, and math.

Acknowledgements

I would like to thank my husband Alden for his patience during the long nights spent alone, for listening patiently to new rhymes, for art ideas shared through the years, and for his wonderful face. I would also like to thank my fellow Linworth author (*Rhymes and Reasons*) and walking partner, Jane Heitman, for her many helpful suggestions and my editor, Sherry York, for her understanding and guidance.

Introduction

WHO NEEDS PHONICS?

Reading is the keystone of modern culture. It is one of the building blocks of freedom. A person with weak reading skills is likely to have limited choices throughout his life. Reading opens doors, not only to professional achievement, but also to a vast treasure trove of literary art amassed over centuries. Stories, myths, legends, plays, and poems are the property of every reader. These masterpieces of the imagination cultivate compassion, foster the consideration of professional ethics, develop critical thinking, and enable creative problem solving. Such skills and qualities are conducive to satisfying lives and effective societies.

How can we help children master reading? An important early step is the introduction of phonics. The word phonics comes from the Greek root, *phon*, meaning sound. In alphabetic systems such as English, written language is the codification of sequential, meaningful sounds. Young decoders must learn to recognize distinct sound units, or phonemes. From the stream of talk, they must be able to pick out the phoneme that distinguishes the word go from the word no.

At the same time, beginners must learn to associate particular sounds with letter symbols. When they have memorized the letter symbols and recognize the most common phonemes, young readers are ready to attack simple consonant-vowel-consonant words. With a shiver of excitement, they will hear themselves say familiar words, and the magical process of reading will begin.

Although a mastery of phonics is crucial, other competencies contribute to reading success. These enabling skills include the ability to concentrate on a task, a broad speaking vocabulary, recognition of similarities and differences (aural, visual, and abstract), the ability to categorize, the ability to think critically, the ability to make reasonable predictions based on known circumstances, and the ability to construct sequences. The arts help to develop these important abilities. That is why visual art, music, dance, and drama activities are included in *ABC, Follow Me!*

BUILDING LANGUAGE AND THINKING SKILLS

- Provide attention-building activities, such as coloring, block play, and computer games.
- Read aloud often.
- Define unusual words.
- Ask what comes next in a story.
- Ask whether a story event seems possible or fair.
- Ask how two things are alike or different.
- Ask participants to list a session's events in order.

WHO NEEDS THIS BOOK?

Written by an experienced classroom teacher and school library language arts specialist, *ABC, Follow Me!* is designed to make the mastery of early reading skills enjoyable. Its rhymes and related art activities capitalize on children's natural enthusiasm for manipulating sounds and shapes.

Although many believe that reading instruction is a responsibility best relegated to the classroom, experienced professionals understand the essential role of school and public librarians in the development of capable, enthusiastic readers. *ABC, Follow Me!* is perfect for school and public libraries. Its verses, movement activities, and simple projects will add extra zip to preschool and primary story hours. As letter recognition skills taught in the poems and crafts are applied to volumes in the library's collection, children will make the connection between phonics and stories. Teaching letter recognition skills in the library is like giving a child a push on the swings; get her started, and soon her toes will touch the clouds.

In *ABC, Follow Me!* classroom professionals are sure to find many easy, lively ways to introduce lessons or reinforce student mastery of particular letter/sound associations. There are activities to suit every child from the budding Wordsworth to the resident wiggle-worm.

Librarians and teachers are important coaches for young readers, but parents are also essential members of the instructional team. Nobody understands a child's unique personality, interests, and needs as well as his family. Most parents, and many grandparents, are eager to help children succeed, but they are not sure where to begin. Family members don't want to make reading into a chore, but they don't want to leave the acquisition of skills to chance, either. *ABC, Follow Me!* offers conscientious mothers and fathers a buffet of simple, enjoyable activities that will carry their children far beyond letter names taught by the ubiquitous ABC song without the intimidating expectations of flashcard drills.

WHAT ARE THE FEATURES OF THIS BOOK?

Each section of *ABC, Follow Me!* considers a different aspect of decoding and is preceded by a short, easy-to-read introduction. In addition to an explanation of the skill taught in that section, each introduction contains some or all of the following:

- suggestions for additional activities
- a short bibliography of related picture books
- a sampling of related teaching materials or relevant Web sites.

OTHER USEFUL FEATURES OF THIS BOOK

- an annotated table of contents
- a list of craft projects
- a reading standards correlation chart
- a word list for additional games or exercises
- an index
- take home activities (for some units)
- flannel board patterns
- alphabet card patterns

A series of teaching units called activities follow the section introduction. Each activity set includes a chant or verse followed by an art or craft project. The activity units also include pattern pages, flannel board patterns, or letter cards. Most of the pattern pages also include take-home suggestions.

WHY ARE THE LETTERS INTRODUCED OUT OF ORDER?

The verse/project units in *ABC, Follow Me!* are presented in order of difficulty. Beginning with the memorization of letter symbols, the text moves on to emphasize their sequence, and then to a letter by letter exploration of sounds. The consonants are covered first because, with a few exceptions, each has only one sound. This attribute makes consonants more dependable guides for decoding than vowels. As a practical demonstration of consonant power, try reading each of the following sentences:

Rd ths smpl sntnc
ea i ie eee.

Both groups of letters represent the words, Read this simple sentence. The first line contains only consonants, while the second contains only vowels. Which group of letters provided more useful information?

Glancing at the table of contents, you will notice that the consonants are not presented in order. Some consonants are used frequently and others, especially C and G, are confusing. In the vowel section of the book, short sounds are presented before long sounds because the vowel-consonant-vowel pattern (can) is simpler than the vowel-consonant-vowel-silent E pattern (cane).

Since *ABC, Follow Me!* is intended to supplement other programs, few readers will follow its units in order. Most teachers, parents, and librarians will flip through the pages to find an appealing verse. The table of contents, index, and various content charts should also help users locate material relevant to current projects or interests.

DO THE CRAFTS TAKE ELABORATE PREPARATION AND CLEAN-UP?

The projects in *ABC, Follow Me!* reinforce skills taught in the verses. They are as simple as possible; many have patterns. Most activities require only crayons, glue sticks, and scissors. These cut-and-color crafts make fast and easy projects for library or reading center sessions. For the benefit of classroom teachers with more time for clean-up, suggestions for more creative projects are included.

Each craft page includes:

- a photograph of a completed sample
- a list of materials
- bulleted instructions
- suggestions for related art activities

A FINAL WORD

However it is used, *ABC, Follow Me!* is meant to infuse early reading instruction with the spirit of childhood. This book is for teachers, parents, librarians, and media specialists who believe that children learn best when they are having fun.

USEFUL WEB SITES

The following education-related index sites are guides to the best on the Internet. They will save you a great deal of time. In addition to lesson plans and activity suggestions, they include professional development and job placement advice.

Kathy Schrock's Guide
>>*http://school.discovery.com/schrockguide/*

> Author and lecturer Kathy Schrock has assembled a comprehensive, categorized guide to sites "useful for enhancing curriculum and professional growth." The fact that it is well-maintained and updated frequently makes this one of the most trusted indexes online.

Sites for Teachers
>>*http://sitesforteachers.com/index.html*>>

> This massive site provides links to, and reviews of, a variety of teaching materials, arranged by subject.

Elementary Educators at About.com
>>*http://k6educators.about/*>>

> At About.com, moderators with experience in a variety of fields select relevant sites for particular purposes. The site listings are updated regularly. Sometimes, moderators also write introductions brimming with useful information. A free newsletter is available.

Art Project List

These crafts are designed to build sound recognition. They also teach basic art elements and principles. Most of the activities listed here are based on included patterns. Suggestions for more time-consuming, open-ended projects are also included, at the bottom of most instruction pages.

Alphabet Crowns	7-9
Alphabet Chains	17-18
Masks	23-25
Suns	27-28
T is for Tie	30-31
Hand Tracings: Holding Rainbows	33
Keys	36-37
B Books	39-40
Funny Faces	44 and 25 (features)
Paper Lantern	45-46
N is for Nature	49-50
Dino-rama	53-54
Weaving with Paper	57-59
Color Wheel	61-62
Goofy Goggles	65-66
Paper Jewelry	68-69
Rattle Bottle	71-72
Paper People	75-76
Vegetable Prints	79-80
Yellow Leaves, Yellow Trees	83
Zigzag Books	87-88
Quilt Blocks	90-91
Wax Resist	94
Middle Rabbit	96-97
C-V-C Bugs	103-104
Flat Bat	106-107
Red and Green	109-110
Go Fish	112-113
Blob Art	116-117
Cut Paper	119-120
Long Vowel Project	121-122
Cut Paper Snake	125-126
Kite Bookmarks	129-130
Drawing Home	132
White Clouds in a Blue Sky	134

Standards Correlation Chart

Addresses State Standards Related to:

Upper case letter symbols 5-18, 21-31, 68-69
Lower case letter symbols 10-18, 31, 40
Alphabetical sequence 5-18
Initial consonant sounds 5-9, 19-91
Medial consonant sounds 91-97
Long vowel sounds 121-134
Short vowel sounds 99-120
Rhyming words 5-136
Listening to stories and poems 5, 10, 16, 21, 26, 29, 32, 34, 39, 42-43, 45,
    49, 52, 55, 60, 64, 67, 71, 74, 78, 82, 86, 89, 92, 95, 101, 102, 105, 108, 111, 115, 118, 121,
    124, 127, 131, 133
Learning verses 5, 10, 16, 21, 26, 29, 32, 34, 39, 42-43, 45,
    49, 52, 55, 60, 64, 67, 71, 74, 78, 82, 86, 89, 92, 95, 101, 102, 105, 108, 111, 115, 118, 121,
    124, 127, 131, 133
Dramatizing poems (drama) 5, 10, 16, 21, 26, 29, 32, 34, 39, 42-43, 45,
    49, 52, 55, 60, 64, 67, 71, 74, 78, 82, 86, 89, 92, 95, 101, 102, 105, 108, 111, 115, 118, 121,
    124, 127, 131, 133
Creating and sharing original art (art) 14, 17, 23, 27, 30, 33, 37, 40, 44, 46, 50, 53,
    61, 65, 68, 72, 75, 80, 83, 87, 96, 103, 106, 109, 112, 116, 119, 122, 125, 132, 134
Copying sound patterns (music) 5, 10, 16, 21, 26, 29, 32, 34, 39, 42-43, 45,
    49, 52, 55, 60, 64, 67, 71, 74, 78, 82, 86, 89, 92, 95, 101, 102, 105, 108, 111, 115, 118, 121,
    124, 127, 131, 133

SECTION 1
The Alphabet: Symbols and Sequence

INTRODUCTION

I learned to drive when I was 30. It was a humbling and confusing experience, but it opened up my life and set me free in ways I could not have imagined. Like driving, reading builds independence. Also, like driving, reading involves many separate skills. At first, a new driver must concentrate on each step. Steering, shifting, and braking must be accomplished while watching traffic, estimating distances, and remembering rules. Once learned, these complex behaviors integrate seamlessly, but at first, they are daunting.

The new reader faces a similarly baffling set of challenges. Before he can began to read a child must memorize 26 letter names in order. More important, he must recognize both upper and lower case letter symbols. Most vital of all, he must understand that letters represent sounds. Three activities in the first section of *ABC, Follow Me!* address these important skills.

Activities

■ *ABC, Follow Me*

The title verse of *ABC, Follow Me!* is designed to help students associate letters with sounds. In this action rhyme, students learn that the word apple begins with an a. The rhyme suggests motions. Read it through before you begin, and decide how to adapt the movements to your personality, your group, and your space.

Following the rhyme, there is a simple color-and-cut activity. Because children enjoy ruling their kingdoms, the first craft in this book is a crown. With your help, each prince or princess will use a crayon to print his or her initial on the crown and then embellish it with colorful jewels.

■ Upper and Lower Case

This rhyme, accompanied by distributable cards, encourages audience participation as it teaches the relationship between upper and lower case letters.

The craft that accompanies "Upper and Lower Case" features graphite rubbing. The sample uses an upper and lower case H because those letters are easy for children to cut. If you have a learning center, you may wish to create a full set of "magic" letters for students to reveal. Simply enlarge each of the cards on the reproducible sheets that accompany this lesson. For additional textural interest, letters may be cut from sandpaper, corduroy, or canvas.

■ Before, After, Between

The third rhyme in the book, "Before, After, Between," focuses on the order of letters. Taking a step past the Alphabet Song, the verse encourages children to think about sequence within isolated groups of letters.

The craft accompanying "Before, After, Between" is a paper chain. Each link has a letter of the alphabet, printed in both upper and lower case. Participants color the mixed-up links, cut them out, and put them in order. Preschoolers and other young learners may be offered links for three or four letters at a time. Older children will enjoy ordering the entire alphabet.

SUGGESTIONS FOR ADDITIONAL ACTIVITIES

- Place a letter on the flannel board. Challenge participants to name it and then use a finger to print it in the air.
- Invite students whose names begin with a certain letter to come to the front. Encourage the group to repeat each name and then the name of the letter.
- Shuffle, then pass out pairs of upper and lower case alphabet cards and encourage children to find their partners.
- Outdoors, assign each child a letter, and then play Red Rover or similar game that usually uses names or numbers.
- Shuffle, then pass out alphabet cards, and encourage children to arrange themselves in order.

SUGGESTED PICTURE BOOKS

Aylesworth, Jim, ill. Stephen Gammell. *Old Black Fly*. New York: Henry Holt and Company, 1992.

Boynton, Sandra. *A is for Angry: An Adjective and Animal Alphabet*. New York: Workman Publishing, 1983.

Campbell, Lisa Ernst. *The Turn-Around, Upside-Down Alphabet Book*. New York: Simon and Schuster Children's Publishing, 2004.

Gerstein, Mordicai. *The Absolutely Awful Alphabet*. San Diego: Harcourt Brace, 1999.

Horenstein, Henry. *Arf! Beg! Catch! Dogs from A to Z*. New York: Scholastic, 1999.

MacDonald, Ross. *Achoo! Bang, Crash! The Noisy Alphabet*. Brookfield, Connecticut: Roaring Book Press, 2003.

Maurer, Donna. *Annie, Bea, and Chi Chi Dolores: A School Day Alphabet.* New York: Orchard Books, 1996.

Ravishankar, Anushka, ill. Christiane Pieper. *Alphabets are Amazing Animals.* Toronto: Hushion House, 2004.

Somme, Kate. *A Very Active Alphabet Book.* London: Marion Boyars Publishers, Ltd., 2006.

Umler, Michael, ill. Mark Braught. *J is for Jump Shot: A Basketball Alphabet.* Chelsea, Michigan: Sleeping Bear Press, 2005.

RELATED TEACHING MATERIALS

Sanders, Nancy. *Read and Write Mini-Books: Beginning Sounds From A to Z: Interactive Stories That Give Early Readers Practice Reading and Writing Words That Begin With...of the Alphabet.* New York: Teaching Resources (Scholastic Professional), 2006.

RELEVANT WEB SITES

"Printable Alphabet Coloring Pages," <<*http://www.learningplanet.com/parents/alphabet/*
A set of illustrated alphabet coloring pages to download.

"ABC Yummy Treat Book," <<*http://www.atozteacherstuff.com/pages/103.shtml*>>.
A tasty lesson to accompany a picture book. Other lessons are also available on this site.

"A Jan Brett Alphabet," <<*http://www.janbrett.com/alphabet/alphabet_main.htm*>>
A charming set of alphabet pages.

"Alphabet Preschool Activities and Crafts," <<*http://www.first-school.ws/theme/alphabet.htm*>>
Activities sorted by letter, designed for preschoolers, but adaptable for school-aged students.

Unit 1: Alphabet Symbols

ABC, Follow Me

Introduce or review letter sounds with this rhyme. Before beginning the rhyme, clap once to one side and then once to the other side. Exaggerate your movements as if keeping time to exciting music at a dance. Encourage the group to join you in clapping. Then say:

A (clap)BC(clap), Fol (clap) low me(clap)!
(Clap to one side and then to the other, and encourage the group to repeat.)

ABC, Follow me!
(Say the next line on your own. Perform the motions slowly and encourage participants to do them with you if they can.)

Hints:
Presenting Action Rhymes:
- Adapt the movements to your personality and to the needs of your audience. If the suggested actions are too confusing for a very young group or too stimulating for the situation, leave them out!
- Customize the verses to fit your program. Break long poems into parts and present the smaller sections on different days.
- Rehearse repeated movements with the group before beginning the verse.
- Take your time with movement verses.

A is for apple. Pick it from a tree. (Reach up and pick an apple. Blow on it and polish it. Then take a bite.)

B is for baseball. Now, pitch it to me. (Hold up your hands as if waiting to catch a ball. Encourage the group to throw an imaginary pitch.)

C is for cup. Let's take a drink. (Drink from a cup.)

D is for dishes. Wash them in the sink. (Pretend to wash dishes and put them in the draining rack.)

(Clap to one side and then to the other) ABC, follow me!

(Participants repeat the refrain. Younger groups may stop here and repeat the first four verses instead of continuing to the end.)

E is for an elephant walking at the zoo (Walk ponderously in place, leaning from side to side, or "walk" by slapping your knees.)

F is for four. That's two plus two. (Hold up two fingers on one hand and two on the other.)

G is for go. Let's drive a car. (Pantomime steering a car.)

H is for hands and here they are. (Hold both hands up, palms facing the group.)

(Clap to one side and then to the other.) ABC, follow me!

ABC, Follow Me continued

(Participants repeat the refrain. Younger groups may stop here and repeat the second four verses instead of continuing to the end.)

I is for ink. Write with a pen. (Pantomime writing.)

J is for jumping out and in. (This can be done by actually jumping, or "jumping" your hands in the air. To get the movement, pretend your hands are grasshoppers hopping.)

K is for kitchen. Let's all cook. (Pantomime pouring and stirring.)

L is for listen and also for look. (Cup your ears, and then make binoculars with your hands.)

(Clap to one side and then to the other. Younger groups may stop here and repeat the third four verses instead of continuing to the end.)

ABC, follow me! (Participants repeat the refrain.)

M is for magic. Pull a rabbit from a hat. (Pantomime waving a wand, then pulling a rabbit out of a hat. Look surprised.)

N is for night and here's a bat. (Flap your arms as if flying. For extra giggles, put your upper teeth over your lip.)

O is for odd. What a strange face! (Make a silly expression.)

P is for putting something in its place. (Pantomime putting something on a high shelf)

(Clap to one side and then to the other. Younger groups may stop here and repeat the fourth set of four verses instead of continuing to the end.)

ABC, follow me!

(Participants repeat the refrain.)

Q is for quiet. Put a finger to your lips. (Put a finger to your lips.)

R is for rain. Here's how it drips. (Wiggle your fingers while moving your arms downward.)

S is for sailing on a summer sea. (Make a wave motion with your hands.)

T is for talking. Now, chat with me. (Make "puppets" with your hands and "talk" to the group.)

(Clap to one side and then to the other. Younger groups may stop here and repeat the fifth set of four verses instead of continuing to the end.)

ABC, follow me!

U is for up. Now point that way. (Point up.)

V is for violin. Can you play? (Pantomime playing a violin.)

W is for winter. Feel the chill. (Pantomime shivering. Fold your arms and rub them as if trying to warm up.)

X is for X-ray. Now hold still. (Sit or stand up straight, and stay still.)

Y is for yes. Just nod and smile. (Nod and smile.)

Z is for zoom around a while. (The group can do this, literally, if nobody is downstairs, or just "zoom" with one hand and then the other. If desired, accompany the zoom with a *zzzzzz* sound effect.)

Y is for You and M is for Me

These paper crowns are easy to make and wear. To make them fancier, add glitter glue, sequins, or gems cut from colored gift foil, but crayons and imagination alone work wonders. For inspiration, share pictures of actual historic or contemporary crowns.

Materials:
- copies of an initial crown pattern
- a sample finished crown
- crayons
- scissors
- a stapler
- colored gift foil, sequins, glitter glue (optional)

Figure 1.1
A Crown Photograph

Procedure:

- Invite students to say their names.
- Encourage the group to identify the first letter of each name.
- Distribute copies of the crown pattern.
- Tell each student to copy the first letter of his name in the rectangle on the crown.
- Encourage each student to color the rest of the crown.
- Tell participants to cut out the crown and both strips.
- Staple each letter band to one side of the crown.
- Fit the crown and then staple the two bands together in the back.

From the Studio:

Add sequins or jewels cut from paper-backed gift wrap foils to make the crowns sparkle.

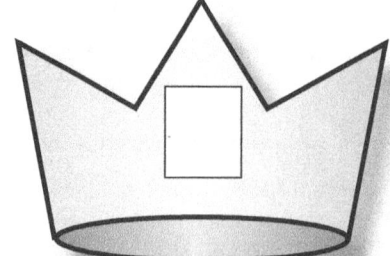
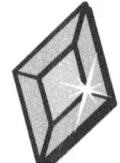

An Initial Crown Pattern

Figure 1.2 A Crown Patter

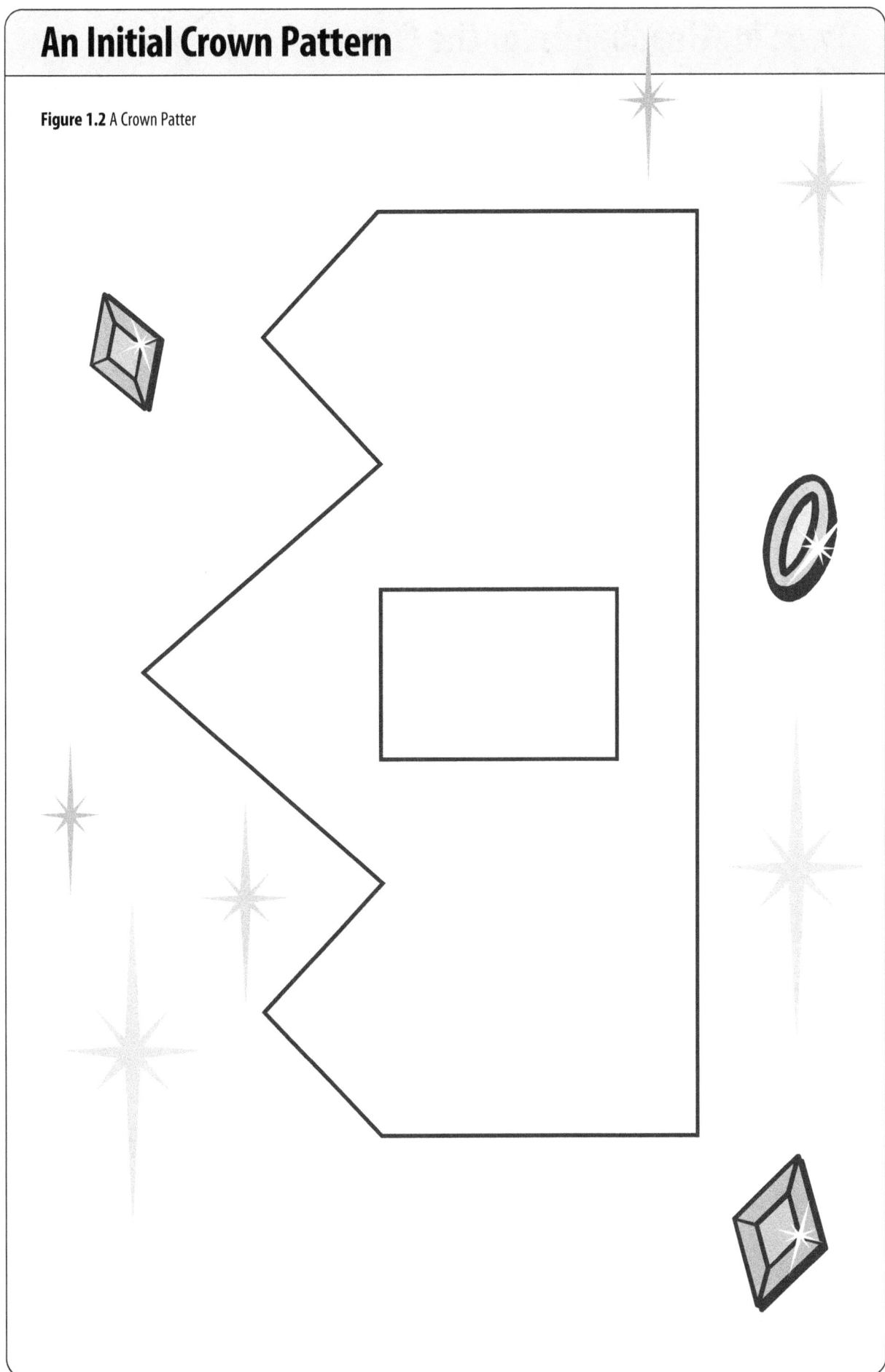

ABC, Follow Me! Phonics Rhymes and Crafts, Grades K-1

Two Side Headbands for the Crown with Upper and Lower Case Letters

Figure 1.3 Two Strips with letters

Unit 2: Upper Case and Lower Case Letters

UPPER CASE AND LOWER CASE: A SHAPE-SHIFTING VERSE

Divide the group into two parts. You may do this by gender, by left and right halves of the room, or by rows. Next, rehearse the poem. Say each line and challenge a section of students to repeat it after you. Then invite the group to perform the entire verse. When the recitation is successful for one letter, move on to the next. Preschoolers and other beginners will spend at least a day on each letter. To review the alphabet in a week, do five letters Monday through Thursday, and six on Friday. Alternate groups so each has a chance to be upper case. Although the letter sounds are introduced, they do not have to be mastered at this point. There is an individual poem for each letter later on in the book.

Since this exercise is about symbol forms, its success depends on participants seeing actual upper and lower case letters. The simplest way to do this in a classroom is to write the letters on the whiteboard or chalkboard. Print each letter as participants say the line. In the library or a meeting room without a board, try using an easel with chart paper and a watercolor marker.

Other display choices include flannel boards or magnetic boards. To make flannel board letters, use the letters on the reproducible cards as patterns. Enlarge them on a copy machine to a size that suits your space; large rooms will require bigger letters than intimate story circles. Next, trace and cut each letter out of colorful felt. Parent volunteers are often willing to help with a task like this.

To make a set of magnetic cards, enlarge each one, laminate it for durability, and then add an adhesive strip magnet (available in craft stores) to the back. This is a lot of work, but you will do it only once. If you don't have volunteers to help, a group of teachers can pool their labor and share the finished set. If funds are available, ready-made felt and magnetic letter sets may be purchased from school supply companies. They have many uses, and are an excellent investment.

Upper Case, Lower Case, Our Names are the Same!

(Write an upper case A on the board, or chart.)

Boys: (Loudly) I am upper case and A is my name.

(Write a lower case a on the board, or chart.)

Girls: (Softly) I am lower case and a is my name.

Boys: (Loudly) Upper case. Girls: (Softly) Lower case.

All: Our names are the same. A!

(Write an upper case B on the board, or chart.)

Girls: (Loudly) I am upper case and B is my name.

(Write a lower case b on the board, or chart.)

Boys: (Softly) I am lower case and B is my name.

Girls: (Loudly) Upper case.

Boys: (Softly) Lower case.

All: Our names are the same. B!

(Write an upper case C on the board, or chart.)

All: (stand) I am upper case and C is my name.

(Write a lower case c on the board, or chart.)

All: (sit): I am lower case and C is my name.

All: (stand) Upper case.

All: (sit): Lower case. Our names are the same. C!

(Write an upper case D on the board, or chart.) Left side of room: (both arms up) I am upper case and D is my name. (hands in lap)

(Write a lower case d on the board, or chart.) Right side of room: (both arms down) I am lower case and D is my name. (hands in lap)

All: (both arms up) Upper case

All: (both arms down) Lower case. Our names are the same. D!

More practice: After all of the letters have been covered, shuffle a group of card pairs (for example, an A card, and an a card.). You will need to divide the number of participants in half to see how many different letters you will cover. For example, a group of 20 would only go up as far as the letter J, the tenth letter in the alphabet. Distribute one card to each participant. Then challenge each card holder to find that letter's partner. Invite each pair of players to stand in turn and name the letter. To cover more letters, repeat the game in another session.

Lower Case Cards

Figure 1.4 Lower Case Cards

Figure 1.4

Upper Case Cards

Figure 1.5 Upper Case Cards

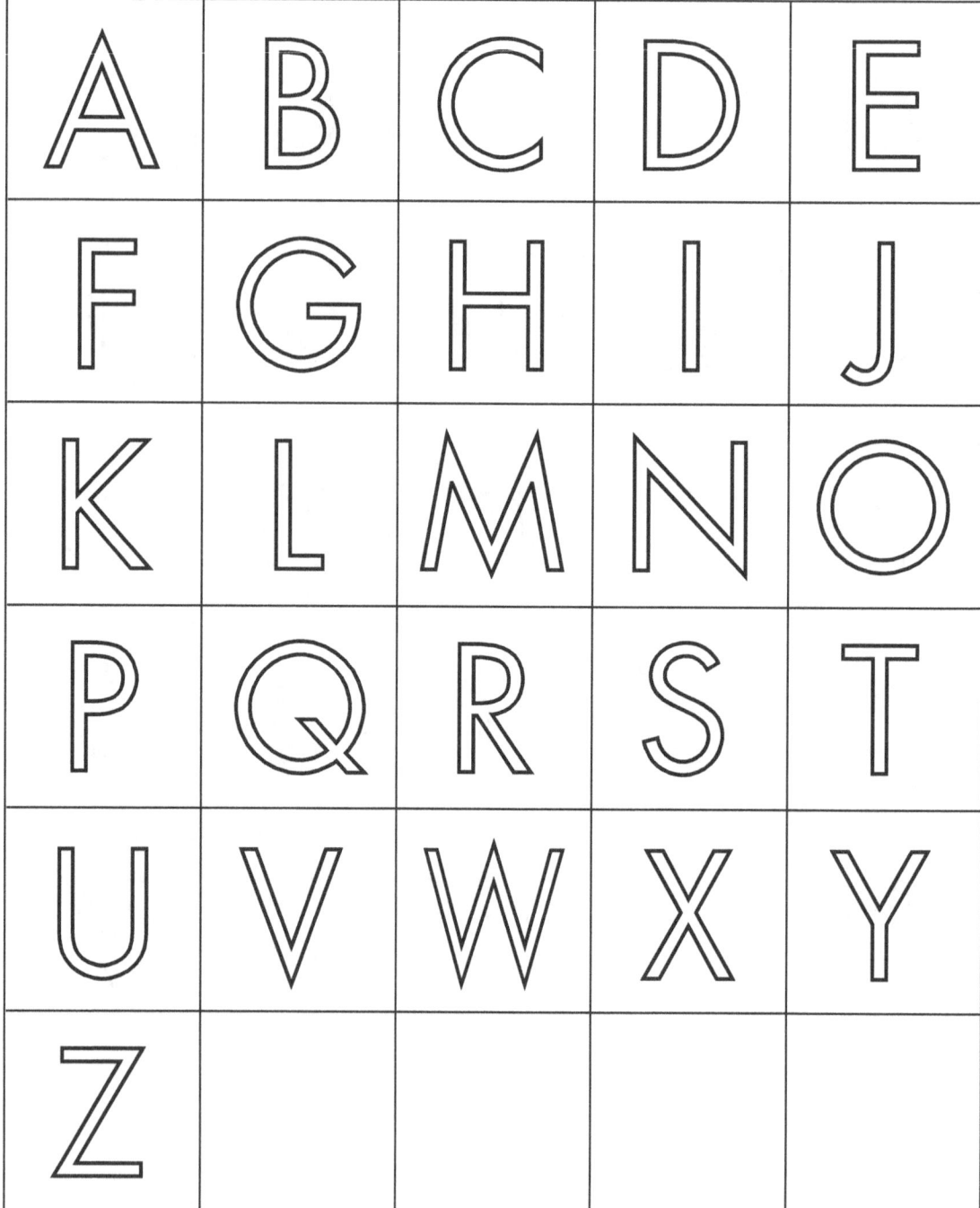

Figure 1.5

Magic Letters

These letters appear like magic on newsprint or any other lightweight paper. You need only pencils, scissors, and copies of Outline Hh. For the letter shapes heavy paper (24 pound, or index weight) is best, but regular copy paper will work. Before the session, make an example with the materials you plan to use.

Materials:
- sharpened graphite or colored pencils (you will be using them on their sides)
- crayons without paper covers (to use instead of pencils)
- scissors
- copies of the Outline Hh page
- blank white paper or newsprint
- a finished example

Figure 1.6 An Hh Rubbing Scan

Procedure:

- Demonstrate how to cut out each letter along the lines. Show what it should look like when complete.
- Help participants with this part of the task, but do not do it for them. Cutting is a good way for children to feel the shape of a symbol.
- Place the cut capital letter on the table.
- Put the blank paper on the top.
- Encourage students to do the same.
- Hold the paper with one hand and rub the paper lightly with the side of the pencil until the letter appears.
- Invite students to make their own rubbings.
- Place the cut lower case letter under the paper and repeat.

From the Studio:
To extend this activity, encourage students to make rubbings with other materials. Several crayon rubbings in different colors may be layered on the same sheet of paper.

Note You may place both letters on the table at once instead of doing them one at a time.

Upper and Lower Case Hh Pattern

Figure 1.7 An Hh Rubbing Pattern

At Home

Find an old catalogue or some junk mail. Cut out some H's and some h's. Paste them to this page.

Unit 3: Alphabet Sequence

PUTTING THE ALPHABET IN ORDER

Alphabetical order is one of those special skills people learn early and use almost every day of their lives. It is also, along with basic counting, one of the first formal examples of sequence. The alphabet song introduces letter names and order, but "Before, After, Between" encourages students to think more specifically about sequence within a given set of letters. It also provides additional practice with letter recognition.

Write the letters on a chart, leaving a space for the missing one, or use felt letters and a flannel board. Add as many verses as you wish. Simply substitute different groups of letters. Because it encourages participants to use clues, this chant goes well with a story hour program that includes detective picture books.

Before, After, Between

A and C, what comes between?

What comes between? What comes between?

ABC; B comes between.

Putting the letters in order.

B and C, what comes next?

What comes next? What comes next?

B C D; D comes next.

Putting the letters in order.

D and E, what comes before?

What comes before? What comes before?

C, D, E; C comes before.

Putting the letters in order.

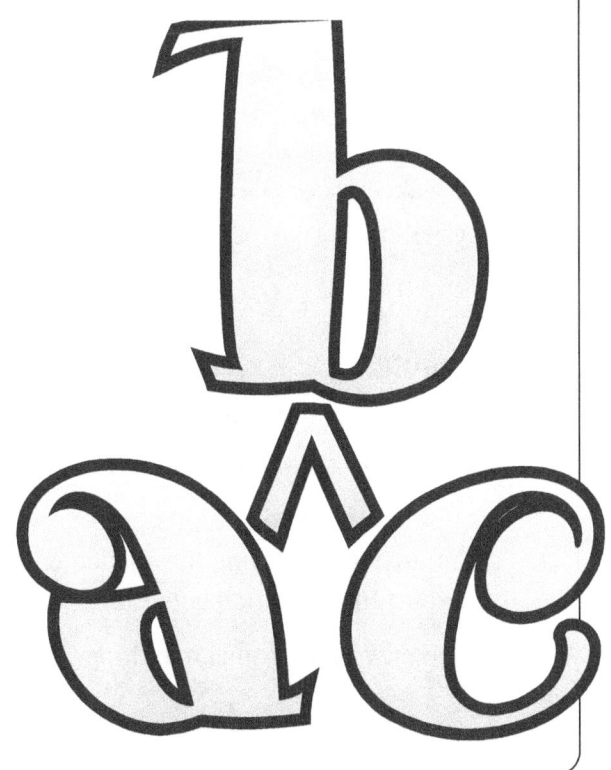

Alphabet Chains

Paper chains are a favorite holiday craft. Here is a variation that can be used at any time of the year. It also reviews alphabet symbols and alphabetical order.

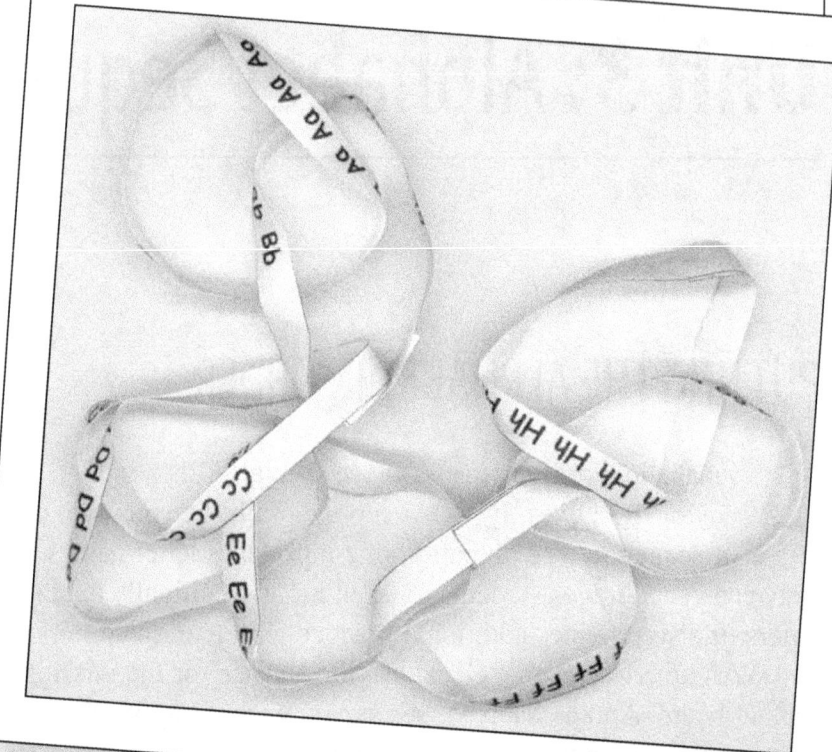

Figure 1.8 A Photograph of an Alphabet Chain

Materials:
- copies of Alphabet Strips page
- scissors (Strips may be cut on a paper cutter in advance. Each full set may be kept together in a standard number ten envelope, or letter strips may be distributed one at a time in order, depending on the skill level of the group.)
- crayons, colored pencils, or nontoxic watercolor markers (If strips are cut in advance, they will be hard to color. Consider duplicating them on tinted paper, instead.)
- glue sticks

From the Studio:
To extend this activity, take students outdoors. Give each participant a letter card and a piece of chalk. Invite group members to work together to write the alphabet in order on the pavement. Encourage them to use large arm movements.

Procedure:

- Distribute copies of the alphabet chain pattern or precut strips. (To make this even easier, limit the number of letters used to five or six.)
- If not duplicated on colored paper, encourage students to color the strips. Caution them to avoid coloring the shaded end of each strip. (Paste or glue will not stick to crayon.) Invite participants to loop the cut strips together in alphabetical order.
- More advanced groups may loop Z into A to create a necklace.

Alphabet Chain Pattern Page

	Aa Aa Aa Aa Aa Aa Aa Aa
	Bb Bb Bb Bb Bb Bb Bb Bb
	Cc Cc Cc Cc Cc Cc Cc Cc Cc
	Dd Dd Dd Dd Dd Dd Dd Dd
	Ee Ee Ee Ee Ee Ee Ee Ee
	Ff Ff Ff Ff Ff Ff Ff Ff
	Gg Gg Gg Gg Gg Gg Gg Gg
	Hh Hh Hh Hh Hh Hh Hh Hh
	Ii Ii Ii Ii Ii Ii Ii Ii Ii Ii
	Jj Jj Jj Jj Jj Jj Jj Jj Jj
	Kk Kk Kk Kk Kk Kk KK KK Kk
	Ll Ll Ll Ll Ll Ll Ll Ll Ll Ll Ll
	Mm Mm Mm Mm Mm Mm Mm
	Nn Nn Nn Nn Nn Nn Nn Nn
	Oo Oo Oo Oo Oo Oo Oo Oo
	Pp Pp Pp Pp Pp Pp Pp Pp Pp
	Qq Qq Qq Qq Qq Qq Qq
	Rr Rr Rr Rr Rr Rr Rr Rr Rr
	Ss Ss ss Ss Ss Ss Ss ss Ss
	Tt Tt Tt Tt Tt Tt Tt Tt Tt
	Uu Uu Uu Uu Uu Uu Uu Uu
	Vv Vv Vv Vv Vv Vv Vv Vv Vv
	Ww Ww Ww Ww Ww Ww Ww
	Xx Xx Xx Xx Xx Xx Xx Xx
	Yy Yy Yy Yy Yy Yy Yy Yy
	Zz Zz Zz Zz Zz Zz Zz Zz

Figure 1.9 Alphabet Strip Patterns

At Home
Cut out the alphabet strips. Make a chain with the letters of your name.

SECTION 2
Consonants

INTRODUCTION

In this section of *ABC, Follow Me!*, each consonant has its own verse and art activity. Specific teaching suggestions precede each activity. Here are some additional ideas and resources for reinforcing consonant skills.

■ ***Select a Consonant of the Day.***
Make up several riddles that can be answered by words starting with the chosen consonant. Here is an example: I have reddish fur. I am very clever. I look like a dog, but I am wild. My name starts with an F. What am I?

■ ***Read a big book to the group.***
Challenge group members to find a certain consonant, such as an M on the page.

■ ***Put a group of items in a bag.***
Encourage a volunteer to pull out one of them. Invite the group to identify the item and the consonant that begins its name. A variation on this is to use a theme bag. For example, an old purse might contain a pencil, a pen, and a picture.

■ ***Adapt one of the poem or craft ideas for use with a different consonant.***
For example, if only M items can be seen in a magic mirror, what might be reflected?

Hints:
Although alliterative titles are obvious choices for consonant themes, other picture books may be equally valuable. Simply point out a featured letter when you reach it in the reading. For example, the book *Rotten Teeth* by David Catrow might serve for either R or T, and *Zeke Pippin*, a delightful tale by William Steig, might be used for Z, P or even H, because the story involves a harmonica. If there is time, read short books again very slowly, encouraging students to raise their hands every time they hear the targeted consonant.

Suggested Picture Books:

Here are some delightful stories. Some have alliterative titles, and others do not.

Henkes, Kevin. *Lilly's Purple Plastic Purse.* New York: Greenwillow, 1996.

O. Tunnell, Michael, ill. Ted Rand. *Mailing May.* New York: Greenwillow, 1997.

Rosenberg, Liz, ill. Stephen Gammell. *Monster Mama.* New York: Philomel, 1993.

Simms, Laura, ill. David Catrow. *Rotten Teeth.* Boston: Houghton Mifflin, 1998.

Stanley, Diane, ill. G. Brian Karas. *Saving Sweetness.* New York: Putnam's Sons, 1996.

Steig, William, *Zeke Pippin.* New York: HarperCollins, 1994.

Relevant Web sites:

Internet4Classrooms, Interactive Sites:
<<*http*://www.internet4classrooms.com/skills_1st.*htm*>>. This is a great directory of online teaching games and other activities, arranged by subject, and well maintained.

Early Reading Skills
<<*http*://www.okaloosa.k12.fl.us/south/early_reading_skills.*htm*>>. Links to useful online activities and printable sheets are featured at this site, which is arranged by reading skill.

Unit 1: M

M is for Moth

In this action rhyme, participants learn to recognize the sound of the consonant M. Whenever you say M, hold your hands at chest height, palms facing each other, and curl all of the fingers inward. Bring both sets of fingers together to make a lower case M.

M is for a moth on a misty night. (Form the M.)

Flitting all around in soft moonlight. (Make small waving motions with the fingers of one hand, and then the other to simulate a moth's flight.)

M is for a moose, high on a hill. (Form the M.)

Now, he is walking; now, he is still. ("Walk" by tapping alternate knees with your palms. Stop on still.)

M is for mule, as stubborn as can be. (Form the M.)

Sometimes I am as stubborn as he. (Cross your arms and glower.)

M is for monkey, swinging around. (Form the M.)

Listen to me make a monkey sound. (Imitate a monkey.)

M is for meerkat, peeking from a hole. (Form the M.)

Is he a prairie dog; is he a mole? (Shake your head no.)

M is for margay, a tropical cat. (Form the M.)

What is he hunting? A tropical rat? (Imitate a cat stalking. Curl your fingers downward, to suggest paws. Lift one hand, and then the other, stealthily.)

M is for manatees, grazing in the bay. (Form the M.)

They eat and they rest, and sometimes they play. (Act out each action word. For "eat," just make chewing motions, for rest, tilt your head and close your eyes briefly, for play, do a

**Hints:
Presenting
Action Rhymes:**
Before presenting an action verse, help participants rehearse the movements. Don't make them practice too long. Some imperfection adds to the fun. After you say each line and do the action, wait for the group to join you.

small action that suggests performing a barrel roll in the water. For example, move both hands and your head in a circle.)

M is for marmot, near a high peak. (Form the M.)

Munching on daisies down by the creek. (Pretend to pick a flower, eat it, and then rub your tummy.)

M is for mudpuppy hiding in the sand. (Form the M.

On the pond bottom, never on land. (Pretend to swim underwater.)

M is for mice in a mossy nest. (Form the M.)

Mother is out. Lie still and rest. (Put palms together to make a pillow and rest your head.)

M is for mastodons, moonrats, and men. (Form the M.)

Now, can you make that M again?

M is for Mask Art Project

Masks are exciting forms of art. People have been creating them for thousands of years. Before beginning this project, share pictures of African, Native American (First Nations), or Asian masks.

Materials:
- copies of the M mask pattern
- markers
- scissors
- yarn
- a sample M mask (Make this in advance.)

Figure 2.1 Picture of a Finished Mask

Procedure:

- Review the letter M and invite students to name some M words.
- Show students your sample M mask. Explain that it is a mask. Hold it up to your face.
- Hold up the blank letter M mask pattern. Invite students to identify the letter.
- Tell students that the word mask begins with an M. Encourage them to repeat the word, emphasizing the M sound.
- Ask students what their mask might represent. Suggest birds, animals, and people.
- Demonstrate how to add a nose and eyes with markers.
- Distribute the markers and copies of the outline letter M.
- Encourage students to add details.
- Distribute scissors and encourage participants to cut out their masks.
- Punch holes in the spots marked on the handout.
- Add yarn ties.

From the Studio:

Other M art and craft projects include cut paper mosaics and monoprints, single prints made by pressing a sheet of paper to wet finger paintings or similar transferable artwork.

M is for Mask Pattern

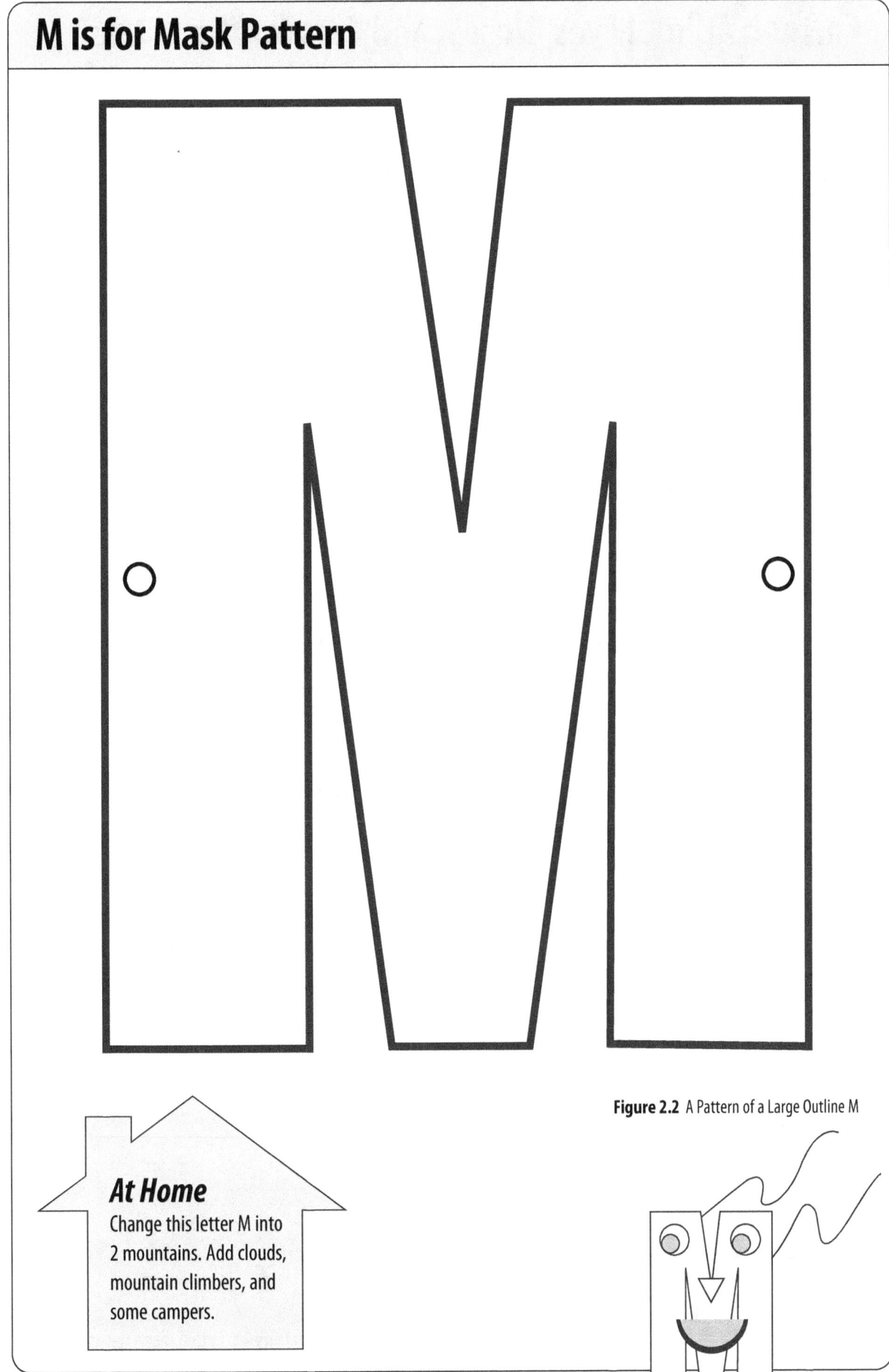

Figure 2.2 A Pattern of a Large Outline M

At Home
Change this letter M into 2 mountains. Add clouds, mountain climbers, and some campers.

Cartoon Animal Eyes, Noses, and Ears for the M Mask

At Home
Use the back of this page. Draw a square. That is the face. Choose an eye shape. Draw 2. Add a nose, a mouth, ears, and hair. Who is this? Tell someone a story about your character.

Figure 2.3 Cartoon Animal Eyes and Noses

Unit 2: S

S IS FOR THE SUN

Introduce this poem with several picture books about the solar system or space travel. Possibilities include *Max Goes to the Moon: A Science Adventure with Max the Dog* by Jeffrey Bennett, *Postcards from Pluto* by Loreen Leedy, *Solar System* by Gregory Vogt, and *Stargazers* by Gail Gibbons. Ask participants to imagine what it would be like to take a trip to another planet. Encourage them to join you in a countdown, and in making blast-off sounds. Next, either show or write the letter S. Then, present the poem.

S is for Sun

Leader: S is for sun.

Participants: S is for sun.

Leader: S is for star.

Participants: S is for star

Leader: and the sky that's above you wherever you are.

Leader: S is for science.

Participants: S is for science.

Leader: S is for space.

Participants: S is for space

Leader: and for the shadows on the moon's face.

Leader: S is for searching.

Participants: S is for searching.

Leader: S is for show.

Participants: S is for show

Leader: and for a station where space shuttles go.

Leader: S is for Saturn.

Participants: S is for Saturn.

Leader: S is for spare.

Participants: S is for spare

Leader: and for the suits that the astronauts wear.

ABC, Follow Me! Phonics Rhymes and Crafts, Grades K-1

Sun Symbols

Discuss the concept of symbols. Give examples. The smiley face is a familiar one. Others include hearts, shamrocks, and arrows. Point out that the sun and moon are not really people, but it is fun to imagine that they are characters. Explain to your artists that they will be using the disk of the sun as a face. Encourage them to look at you, or each other, and notice various facial features they might need. Possibilities include eyes, noses, mouths, eyebrows, eyelids, eyelashes, and lips. Point out that the sun does not have hair, but it does have rays, which may be depicted as wavy lines, zigzags, or straight lines radiating outward. For additional inspiration, share the classic picture book, *Arrow to the Sun: A Pueblo Indian Tale* by Gerald McDermott or show pictures of masks or of sun symbols from the library media collection.

Figure 2.4 Scan of a Finished Sun Symbol

Materials:
- copies of "Sun Symbol Pattern"
- crayons
- pictures of masks

Procedure:

- Introduce the concept of a sun symbol and show pictures of masks.
- Show a sample sun mask.
- Distribute copies of the sun pattern.
- Distribute crayons.
- Hold up various works in progress for inspiration.

From the Studio:
To extend this activity, encourage students to create original moon and planet masks. Each planet should have a separate personality. When the masks are finished, separate the participants into groups and encourage them to create a story using their characters.

Sun Symbol Pattern

At Home
Look in the newspaper. Find words that begin with an S. Cut them out and paste them inside the S circle.

Figure 2.5 Sun Symbol Pattern

Unit 3: T

T IS FOR TRUE

Tell students that they are going to have to think, and then answer together. Have them practice saying "tricky!" and "true" when you point to them. Give the first line as an example.

Is it Tricky or is it True?

Leader: A dog has a tail and so do you. Is it tricky, or is it true?
Participants: Tricky!
Leader: Tape is sticky and so is glue. Is it tricky, or is it true?
Participants: True!
Leader: Your hair and skin are turquoise blue. Is it tricky, or is it true?
Participants: Tricky!
Leader: Tar is thick: fudge is too. Is it tricky, or is it true?
Participants: True!
Leader: A cat says woof! and a dog says mew! Is it tricky, or is it true?
Participants: Tricky!
Leader: A tadpole lives in an old green shoe. Is it tricky, or is it true?
Participants: Tricky!
Leader: A horse says neigh! and a cow says moo. Is it tricky, or is it true?
Participants: True!
Leader: A penguin waddled and an eagle flew. Was it tricky, or was it true?
Participants: True!
Leader: An artist roared and a lion drew. Was it tricky, or was it true?
Participants: Tricky!
Leader: Tapirs and tigers can live in a zoo. Is it tricky, or is it true?
Participants: True!
Leader: People have teeth to help them chew. Is it tricky, or is it true?
Participants: True!
Leader: One o'clock comes after two. Is it tricky, or is it true?
Participants: Tricky!
Leader: I like stories, and so do you. Is it tricky, or is it true?
Participants: True!

Build critical thinking skills by asking questions about stories and real-life situations.

Examples: Is that possible? Is that fair? How does he know that?

Truly Tricky Ties

Materials:
- copies of "T is for Tie"
- crayons
- scissors
- a sample Truly Tricky Tie
- old ties
- large paperclips (optional)
- stapler and staples (optional)

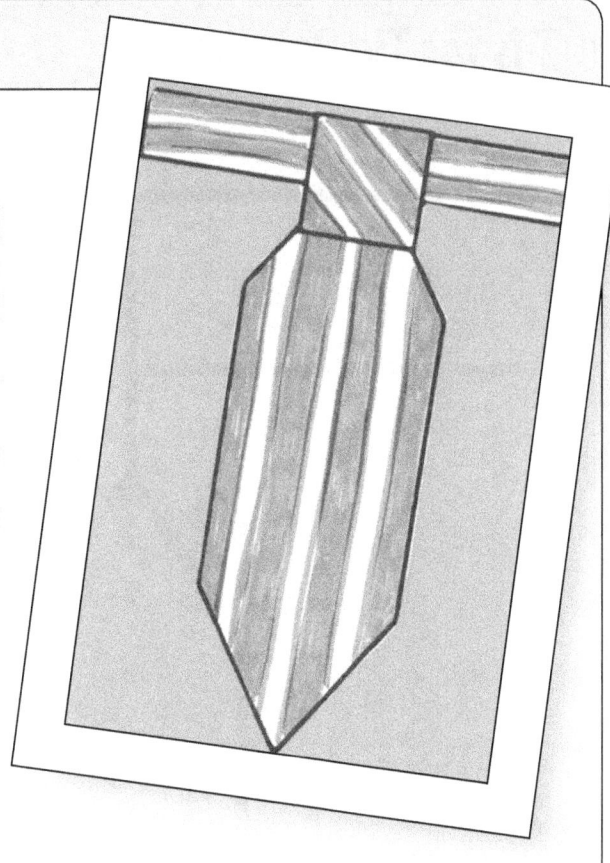

Figure 2.6 A Scanned Finished Necktie

Procedure:

- Display the real ties.
- Encourage students to identify them as ties and to name the letter that stands for the sound at the beginning of the word "tie."
- Write a T on the board or display it. If desired, add lines to change the T into a tie. (See the pattern.)
- Point out that most ordinary ties have ordinary designs. Their decorations include stripes, polka dots, circles, triangles, and sometimes pictures. Add a simple pattern to your tie drawing, if you have made one.
- Tell your young artists that they are going to design Truly Tricky Ties.
- Explain that they can draw anything, as long as it is totally silly. If they draw a dog, it should be blue or green. A horse might have six legs and wings.
- Show your previously finished sample.
- Distribute copies of the tie pattern and crayons.
- When your designers have finished coloring, distribute the scissors.
- Encourage participants to cut out their ties. Paper strips may be stapled to each side of the T's crossbar to make the tie wearable, or it may be attached to a shirt with a large paperclip.

From the Studio:

To expand this project use a double copy of the pattern to make a card for Dad or multiple copies to make a Tie Book. Other T-inspired art activities include tracing and tempera painting.

T is for Tie Pattern

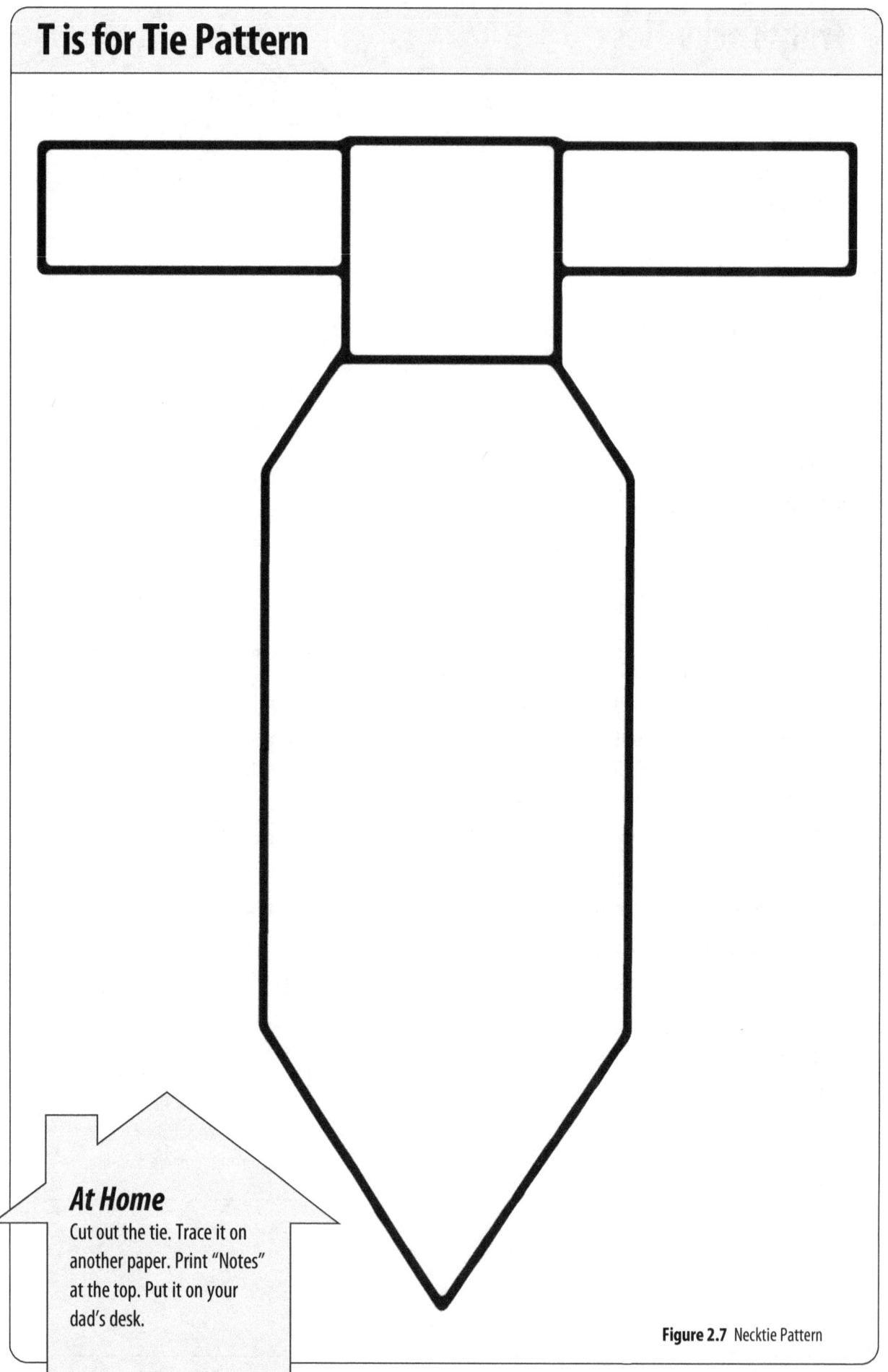

At Home
Cut out the tie. Trace it on another paper. Print "Notes" at the top. Put it on your dad's desk.

Figure 2.7 Necktie Pattern

Unit 4: H

H IS FOR HAND

Bring in an interesting handbag filled with small items, and invite participants to take turns pulling things out of it. Explain that each thing in the bag can be held in one hand. Ask students to look around the room and name some things that cannot be held in one hand, or even two hands. Don't forget the air, or words.

After the discussion, write the letter H on the board and explain that the word hand begins with an H. Ask for the names of other things that begin with an H. Explain that, in the poem, you will name some things that start with H.

After pointing out that the word help begins with H, tell participants that you need theirs.

Explain that you want them to tell you whether or not they could hold an object you describe. Practice by saying, "a hamburger: can you hold it in your hand?" They should say "Yes!" Encourage enthusiastic participation. Next, say "your house: can you hold it in your hand?" They should say "No!" Next, present the following poem:

Can You Hold It in Your Hand?

Leader: Horses galloping along the strand;
Will a horse fit in your hand?
Participants: No!
Leader: Brass horns blaring in school bands;
Can you hold one in your hands?
Participants: Yes!
Leader: Baseball hot dogs, sold at stands;
Can you hold one in your hands?
Participants: Yes!
A little palm hut on tropical sands;
Will that hut fit in your hands?
Participants: No!
Horizon edging sea and land;
Can you hold it in your hand?
Participants: No!

ABC, Follow Me! Phonics Rhymes and Crafts, Grades K-1

Dream Hands

The poem "Can You Hold It In Your Hand?" concentrates on what is possible; it is very down-to-earth. In contrast, the art project "Dream Hands," inspired by surrealist painting, explores a world of imaginative possibilities.

Materials:
- Paper
- crayons
- a study print of a painting by Salvador Dali or any other surrealist painter

Procedure:

- Demonstrate how to trace a hand. Be sure to spread your fingers.

- Ask students what they would like to hold if they could hold anything. Emphasize that for this project, what they hold does not have to be possible in the real world. Participants might be able to grasp their objects only in the imaginary world of wishes or dreams. Give some examples, such as the end of the rainbow, a star, or a heart.

- Tell participants that they will be drawing their wished-for item in the tracing of their hand.

- Show an example that you have made. If you are not a confident artist, try a rainbow, a heart, or a star.

- After participants have finished coloring, they should share their work and explain why they chose the items they did.

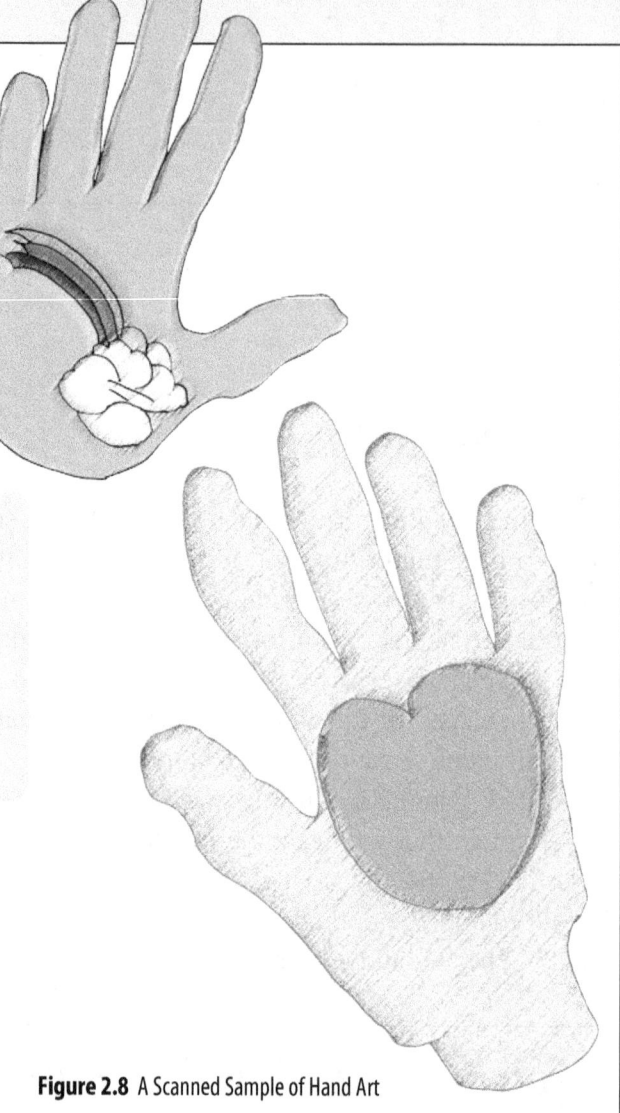

Figure 2.8 A Scanned Sample of Hand Art

From the Studio:

Expand the hand theme by creating a handprint mural with finger paint. For a less messy project, invite students to trace their hands several times on sheets of colored paper and cut them out, then mount them on mural paper. (Available in most schools, mural paper comes on large rolls and is sometimes called colored "bond.") Other H-related art projects include Hot Crayons (crayon shavings ironed between sheets of waxed paper) and Horizons, drawings or paintings of the ocean at sunset, showing the horizon.

Unit 5: K

KEY TO K KINGDOM

The art project "Dream Hands" explored an abstract and imaginative dimension. "K is for Key" continues that theme. In a mythic locale behind a locked gate, there is a world where all spoken words must begin with the letter K. To introduce this verse, place a felt K on a flannel board. Place each object, except the final object, the kiss, on the board in order. Look for enlargeable patterns on the next page.

Instead of using flannel board pieces, you may act out each verse, but be sure to write or display the upper and lower K symbol so children will learn to associate this consonant with its sound.

K is for Key

Leader: There is a place where the words you say
have to begin with the letter K.
There is the lock. Here is the key.
Open the gate, and follow me.

Leader: It's soaring above, at a great height;
it's held on a string. It must be a

Participants: kite.

Leader: In a story they lost their mittens.
They purr. They meow. They must be

Participants: kittens.

Leader: He wears a crown and a royal ring.
He lives in a palace. He must be the

Participants: king.

Leader: It's full of water and made of metal.
Turn on the heat. It is a

Participants: kettle.

Leader: In soccer (football)
this has to be strong and quick.
To make the goal, you can try a

Participants: kick.

Leader: He played, nibbled, chased and hid;
This baby goat is called a

Participants: kid.

Leader: I'll blow you one; I can't miss. (blow a kiss)
Blow one back. It is a

Participants: kiss.

Leader: Here is the lock. Here is the key.
Close the gate and follow me.
We went to a place where the words you say
must begin with the letter

Participants: K.

K is for Key: Flannel Board Patterns or a Coloring Page

At Home
Color the items on the K Flannel Board Patterns page. Draw two things in your house that start with K.

Figure 2.9 K Flannel Board Patterns or a Coloring Page

K is for Key: Clay Impressions

This craft project, best suited for a classroom, allows participants to make a real impression. Make the craft dough ahead of time, and store it in airtight plastic bags. For easy cleanup, give each artist a sheet of waxed paper. There are many excellent craft dough recipes, both in books and on the Internet. The easiest, though not the best, is one part salt, and one part flour. Add water a little at a time, mixing and kneading as you go, until the clay is the consistency of the modeling dough sold in toy stores or very stiff cookie dough.

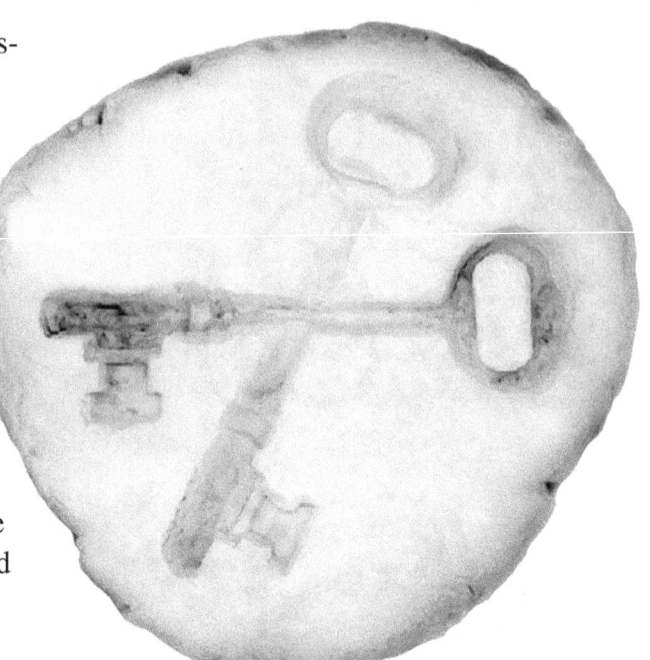

Figure 2.10 A Photograph of a Finished Key Impression

Materials:
- Salt and flour craft dough, commercial craft dough, or clay
- old keys

Procedure:

- Distribute waxed paper sheets.
- Demonstrate how to roll the craft dough into a ball.
- Flatten the ball of dough between your palms.
- Place the dough pancake on the waxed paper and press the key into it.
- Remove the key, leaving an impression.
- Put the finished print on a cookie sheet. Use a self-stick note to add your name.
- The print may take up to a week to dry.
- Distribute the clay and keys.
- Participants complete the project.

From the Studio:
For the library, skip the messy clay. Reproduce the flannel board patterns as a coloring page, make crayon rubbings of keys, or encourage children to draw a magic key and then tell the group what it will open.

Unit 6: B

B IS FOR BOOK

Like "K is for Key," the verse "B is for Book" challenges participants to answer riddles. As you turn the pages of an invisible book, audience members must use clues to guess the "pictures."

B is for Book

Leader: Here is a book that is hard to see.
Everything in it begins with a B.

Leader: Here is someone whose name is Roy.
This is a picture of a happy

Participants: boy!

Leader: Here is something ridden by Mike.
This is a picture of a two-wheeled

Participants: bike!

Leader: These feathered creatures sing without words.
This is a picture of two little

Participants: birds!

Leader: When it rings, you can hear it well.
This is a picture of a schoolhouse

Participants: bell!

Leader: I kicked two of them over a wall.
This is a picture of a rubber

Participants: ball!

Leader: On our last field trip, it carried us.
This is a picture of a yellow

Participants: bus!

Leader: It loves the dark. Imagine that!
This flying mammal is called a

Participants: bat

Leader: Water will flow and ice will melt.
To hold up pants, you need a

Participants: belt!

Leader: Napping in a mountain lair,
this is a picture of a

Participants: bear!

Leader: You have a pillow to rest your head,
and this is a picture of a

Participants: bed!
That was a book that was hard to see,
but everything in it began with a B.
(Print an invisible B in the air.)

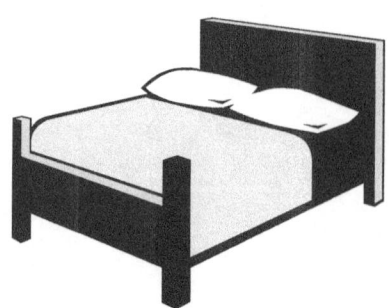

A B Book

Materials:
- copies of Book Pattern
- scissors
- crayons
- a sample B Book

Figure 2.11 A Photograph of a Finished B Book

Procedure:

- Tell students that they have just looked at an invisible B book, and now they are going to make one that is visible.
- Show the sample B book.
- Review the names of some things that start with B.
- Distribute the crayons.
- Encourage students to draw one B object on each page.
- Invite participants to share their finished books.

From the Studio: Encourage students to make similar books for other letters.

A B Book Pattern

At Home
Find an old catalog. Cut out pictures of things that start with B or make a book for another letter. Glue them in the book.

Figure 2.12 A B Book Pattern

Unit 7: F

F IS FOR FUN!

Write a letter F on the board and explain that the word feeling begins with an F. Ask students to name other words that begin with the same sound. Possibilities include fast, find, four, fin, fit, fame, fort, family, fair, fine, and fish. If necessary give riddle clues such as: It swims in the sea. It has fins and gills. It starts with an F. What is it?

Next, ask students to name some things that are fun to do. Ask how they feel when they are having fun. Then, ask them how they feel when they are bored. Explain that you are going to tell them about a situation. Say that you want them to picture themselves in the situation, and then shout out whether it would be boring or fun. Help them practice shouting boring and then fun.

If there is a disagreement, encourage students to explain why they answered the way they did. The responses listed here are only suggestions and not everyone will agree. Critical thinking is a crucial part of the reading process, and this is a good place to begin. If nobody disagrees, at the end of the exercise invite students to think more deeply about the situations in the verse. Challenge them to think of a circumstance under which a hot car trip could be fun or a time when watching fireworks might be boring.

Would it be Boring, or Would it be Fun?

Leader: Riding in a hot car in the summer sun.
Would it be boring, or would it be fun?

Participants: Boring!

Leader: A walk across flat farmland when the drive is done.
Would it be boring, or would it be fun?

Participants: Boring! (probably)

Leader: Riding a rollercoaster on a fast run.
Would it be boring, or would it be fun?

Participants: Fun!

Leader: Visiting a factory with toys by the ton.
Would it be boring, or would it be fun?

Participants: Fun!

Leader: Stopping by a bakery for a sugar bun.
Would it be boring, or would it be fun?

Participants: Fun!

Leader: Watching flashing fireworks when the day is done.
Would it be boring, or would it be fun?

Participants: Fun!

Leader: Running a great race, and being number one.
Would it be boring, or would it be fun?

Participants: Fun!

Leader: Eating a fancy dinner, grownups: 20, children: one.
Would it be boring, or would it be fun?

Participants: Boring!

F is for Funny Face

Figure 2.13 A Picture of a Finished Funny Face

Materials:
- paper plates (not foam)
- markers
- copies of Cartoon Animal Eyes and Noses (See the M is for Mask Unit)
- scissors
- glue
- pictures of clowns

Procedure:

- Show the clown pictures. Ask students to name some places that they might see clowns.

- Point out that the makeup makes the clown's features look bigger. It emphasizes happiness or sadness. Encourage students to make happy and sad faces. Have them watch a partner while making funny faces. Invite them to make observations about the shape of the mouth and the position of the eyebrows. Tell them to use phrases like "turned up," "turned down," or "straight across."

- Explain that clowns use basic shapes like circles and triangles when they design their make-up.

- Show them your sample paper plate funny face.

- Point out some basic shapes from the Cartoon Animal Eyes and Noses page.

- Explain that they will need to copy one mouth, one nose and two eyes. After they draw on the features, they should add silly hair and other details.

> **From the Studio**:
> Other possible F crafts include family pictures, paper plate frogs, and finger painting.

Unit 7: L

LANTERNS, LEOPARDS, AND LAUNCHES

To introduce the letter L, place a felt version on a flannel board. Ask students to raise their left hands. Point out the fact that the word left begins with an L. Then, use the fingers and thumb of that hand to make an L. Hold it out and look at it, turn it around and hold up your left hand so that the fingernails on your L face the students (That move will reverse the letter so it looks correct to your audience.) Then, invite participants to do the same. Tell them to hold up their L's every time they hear a word that starts with the sound they hear at the beginning of left. Read each line slowly, and encourage students to repeat the L word they heard.

Instead of making an L with fingers, you may use cards with the letter L on them. Books about ladybugs, autumn leaves, camping trips, or rainforest animals would be good accompaniments for this poem.

L is for Light

L is for lantern giving us light.
L is for leopard stalking the night.
L's for launching an astronaut hero.
L is for liftoff: Three, two, one, zero!
L is for lake in a mountain valley.
L is for lamp in a city alley.
L's for the lasso that catches a calf.
L is for ladybug, and L's for a laugh.
L's for the ladders that firefighters use,
and L's for leather that's made into shoes.
L is for leg; every lion has four.
L's for the lock that's on our front door.
L is for leaves on summer trees.
L is for lobsters that live in cold seas.
L is for lawn that Dad has to mow.
and L's for the library where new thoughts grow.

L is for Lantern

String some of these festive lanterns and hang them along the top edge of a bulletin board for an easy Asian New Year decoration.

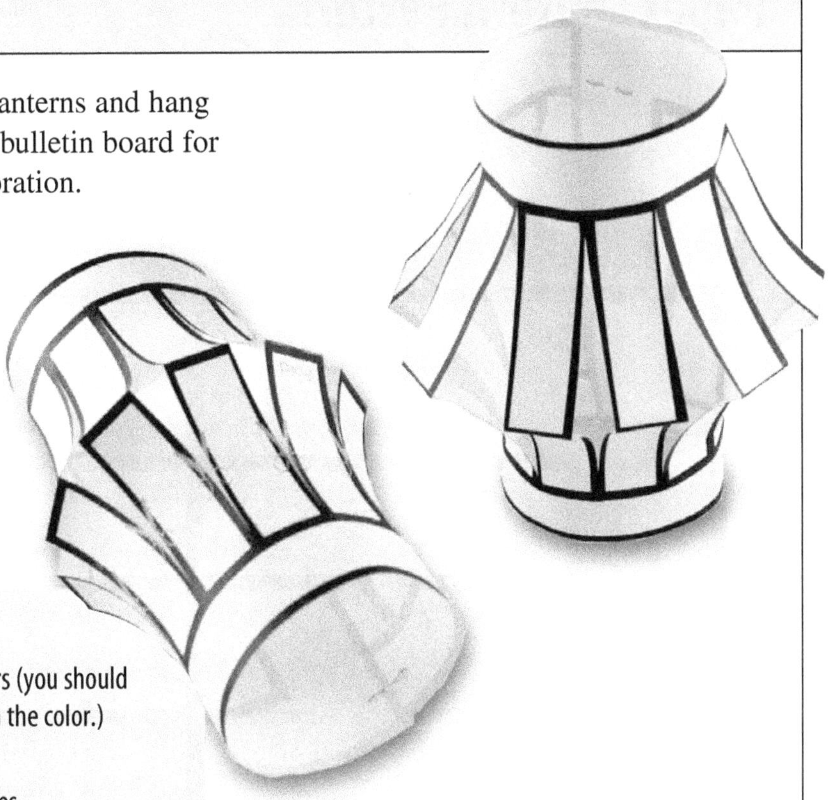

Materials:
- Copy of A Lantern Pattern
- light colored watercolor markers (you should be able to see the lines through the color.)
- scissors
- glue sticks or staplers and staples

Figure 2.14 A photograph of the finished lantern

Procedure:

- Review the sound of L. Encourage students to name some L words from the verse.
- Distribute copies of A Lantern Pattern and markers or crayons.
- Tell students to color the lantern. They may use as many colors as they wish and they do not have to stay inside the lines.
- Cut out the lantern along the heavy edges.
- Fold the lantern in half along the center line. Keep the lines on the outside.
- Start at the fold and cut along the inside parallel lines. Cutting lines are marked with tiny pictures of scissors.
- Unfold.
- Paste or staple the marked side edges together to make a cylinder.
- Push from the top and bottom. The folded edge will bend outward, creating the lantern shape.

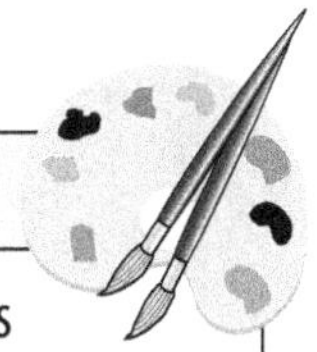

From the Studio:

Additional L art activities include line drawings and letter pictures. To make a letter picture, draw an L, or any other letter, then imagine it to be the beginning of a drawing. For example, an L could be the wall and lower edge of a tall building, or the neck of a giraffe.

Paper Lantern Pattern

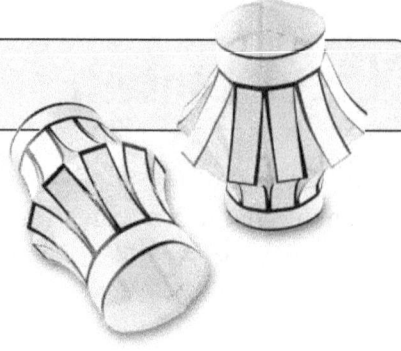

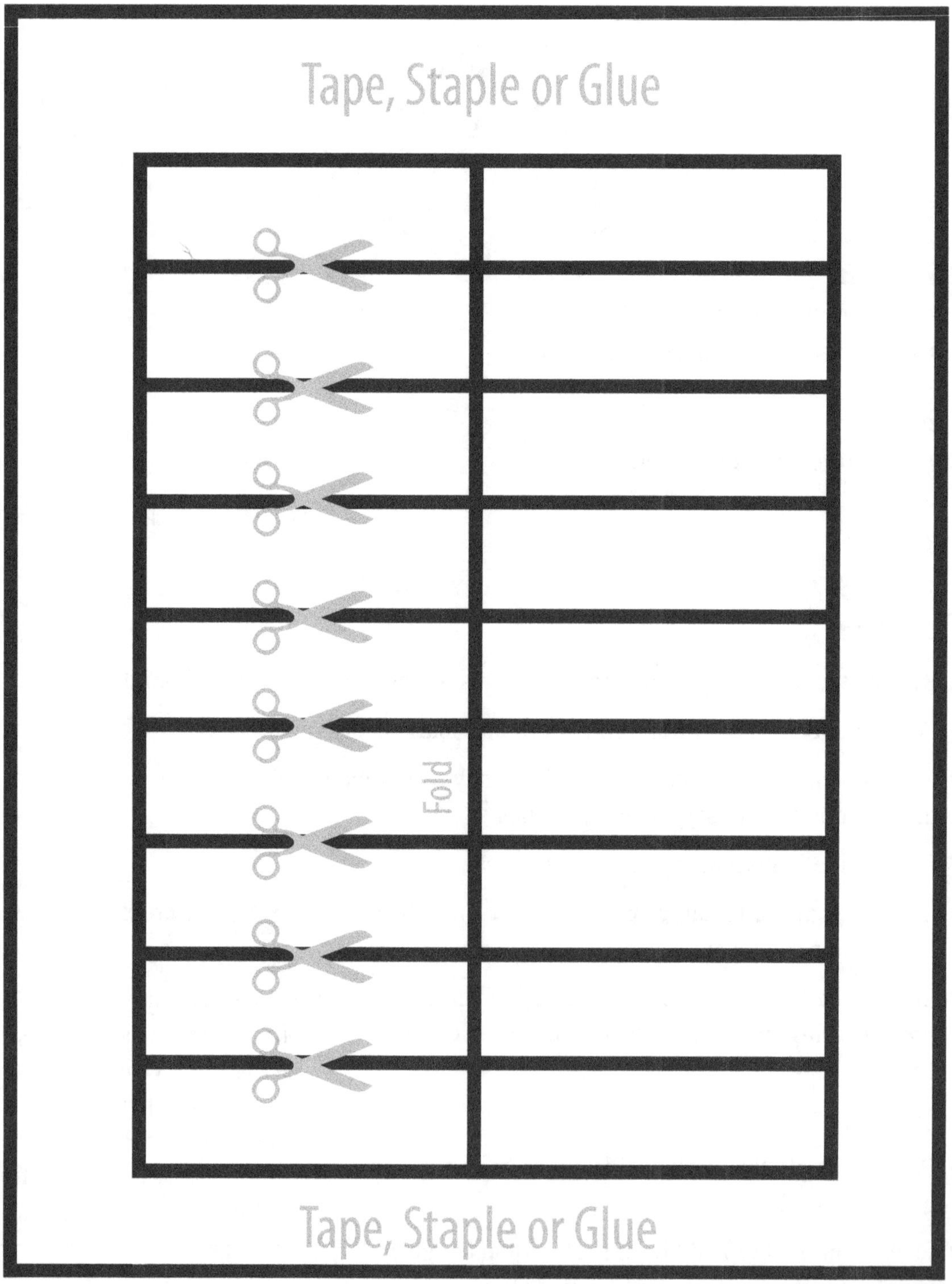

Figure 2.15 A Lantern Pattern

Unit 9: N

NODDING FOR N!

Place the letter N on the flannel board. Say that it begins with the same sound as the word nod. Nod your head and encourage students to join you. Then, explain that the word no also begins with an N. Shake your head from side to side. Tell students that you are going to ask them whether certain words begin with an N. If the word begins with an N, they should nod. If it does not begin with an N, they should shake their heads to show that the answer is no. Help them practice. Then ask:

- Does the word duck begin with an N?
- Does the word noise begin with an N?
- Does the word net begin with an N?
- Does the word turtle begin with an N?

Next, say that you are going to read a verse. Tell participants to listen for words that begin with N. When they hear an N word, they should nod.

N is for Nature

Neptune spinning in the dark,
A bird's nest in the city park,
A native plant beside a stream,
A narrow canyon in a dream,
A newborn fawn among the trees,
A hill of ants, a hive of bees.
The arctic caught in frigid nights,
Lit by glowing Northern Lights,
Ocean dawn and desert noon,
Crater shadows on the moon,
The water where an otter plays,
Star strewn nights and bright, warm days.
A baby's hands, a raccoon's toes,
A nanny goat's eyes, an elephant's nose,
A meadowlark's song, a woodpecker's pecks,
Tortoises' shells and giraffes' long necks,
Wide palm fronds and long pine needles,
Mallards' heads and rainbow beetles,
Numberless acorns and noisy squirrels,
irritated oysters and gleaming pearls,
Where, oh where, can nature be found?
Near and far and all around.
Where, oh where, can nature be?
In neutrons and newts; in you and me.

N is for Nature

If your library or school has a garden, take the group outdoors to find a natural object. If not, collect an interesting group of leaves, stones, shells, and other traceable natural objects. Artificial leaves and bags of shells can be purchased at floral and craft supply outlets.

Tracing the objects improves coordination and builds shape recognition skills. Coloring the overlapped areas creates a new, interesting design.

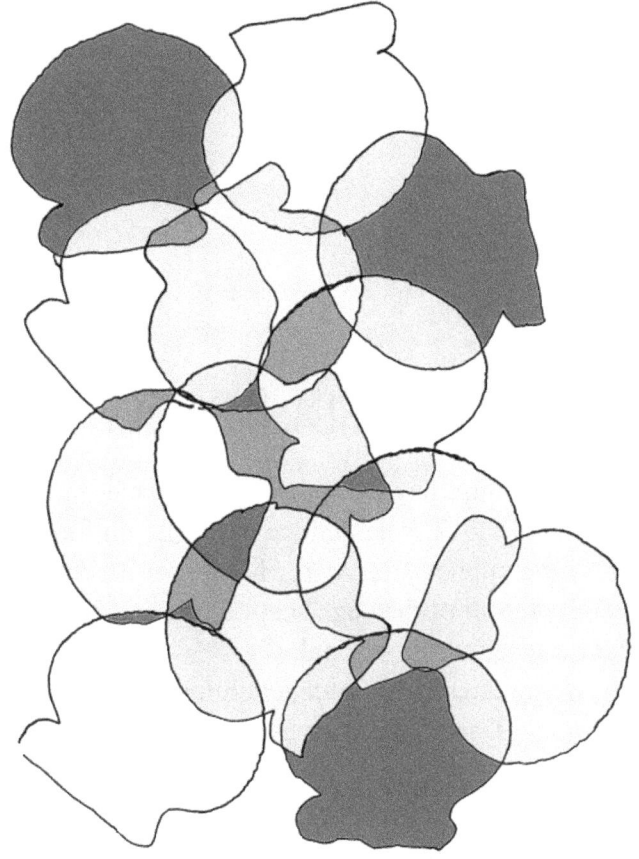

Figure 2.16 A Sample of Traced Nature

Materials:

- stones, leaves, or other natural shapes
- paper
- markers or crayons

Procedure:

- Review the N sound. Encourage students to recall other N words from the verse.
- Encourage each student to choose a natural item and make a tracing.
- Show students how to move the object and trace it again, overlapping the tracings.
- Demonstrate how to color in the spaces where the tracings overlap.
- Repeat to create an interesting composition.
- Encourage students to show their pictures and talk about why they chose their items.

From the Studio:

Other possible nature projects include stone critters (eyes, noses, and whiskers painted on smooth river rocks), leaf prints, and pressed flowers. (Put a fresh flower between two sheets of waxed paper and press the resulting sandwich under a stack of heavy books. For best results, do not disturb for about two weeks).

Unit 10: D

DANNY AND DARLA: D DETECTIVES

You can use any two puppets to present this poem. The only requirement is that one should look male and the other should look female. Animals are fine. If you don't have puppets, find two white paper lunch sacks. Draw big, simple eyes and a nose on the flat bottom of the bag. The folded in section will be the mouth. Yarn or paper strip hair adds bounce, but is optional.

If you have older student volunteers, you might recruit two of them to read the parts of Danny and Darla instead of using puppets. If you have two female helpers, change Danny's name to Danielle.

Before reading the verse, show students the letter D by placing it on the flannel board. Introduce the Danny puppet. Ask participants to think of some words that begin with the same sound as Danny's name. Next, introduce the Darla puppet. Ask what letter is at the beginning of Darla's name. Ask whether anybody in the group has a name that begins with a D.

Explain that Danny and Darla are going to share some puzzlers with them. The boys will answer Danny's clues, and the girls will answer Darla's. Hold up each puppet in turn. Hold up Danny and say, "Boys, who am I?" They should say, "Danny!" Repeat with Darla for the girls.

D is for Detective

Danny puppet: I am Danny the Detective. What do I see? It makes rhythm when you hit it and it starts with a D.
Boys: A drum!

Darla puppet: I am Darla the Detective. What do I see? It's a rock in a ring and it starts with a D.
Girls: A diamond.

Danny puppet: I am Danny the Detective. What do I see? It waddles and it quacks and it starts with a D.
Boys: A duck.

Darla puppet: I am Darla the Detective. What do I see? Yellow center, white petals, and it starts with a D.
Girls: A daisy.

Danny puppet: I am Danny the Detective. What do I see? It says hee haw, and it starts with a D.
Boys: A donkey

Darla puppet: I am Darla the Detective. Whom do I see? Taking care of teeth; a job with a D.
Girls: A dentist.

Danny puppet: I am Danny the Detective. What do I see? It leaps in the waves, and it starts with a D.
Boys: A dolphin

Darla puppet: I am Darla the Detective. What do I see? Water makes it mud, and it starts with a D.
Girls: Dirt.

Danny puppet: I am Danny the Detective. What do I see? It barks and it loves you, and it starts with a D.
Boys: A dog.

Darla puppet: I am Darla the Detective. What do I see? You tie a boat to it, and it starts with a D.
Girls: A dock.

Danny puppet: I am Danny the Detective. What do I see? It's hot, and it's dry, and it starts with a D.
Boys: A desert.

Both puppets: We are Danny and Darla. What do we see? It grazes in a meadow, and it starts with a D.

All: A deer.

D is for Dino-rama

Figure 2.17 A Sample of a Dinosaur Diorama

Procedure:

- Show students the sample dino-rama.
- Share a picture book about dinosaurs, or discuss the fact that dinosaurs were reptiles like lizards and snakes. Explain that we know many things about them, but we do not know what color they were.
- Encourage students to color the base and the dinosaurs.
- Then, have them cut out each shape along the lines.
- Show them how to fold the tabs.
- Demonstrate how to glue the dinosaurs and plants to the green base.
- Invite them to draw and add dinosaurs of their own.

Materials:
- copies of the Dino-rama Pattern
- a finished example of a dino-rama
- green construction paper
- colored watercolor markers
- scissors
- glue stick

From the Studio:
Create craft clay dinosaurs and prehistoric trees made from rolled and cut newspaper. Paint your models with tempera. Tape a video tour of your Dino-rama.

A Dino-rama Pattern

Figure 2.15 A Dino-rama Pattern

Unit 11: W

What Goes in the Wagon?

Leader: This is the W wagon.

Participants: This is the W wagon.

Leader: If you start with a W, Welcome aboard!

Leader: I'm a horse, a horse, a happy horse.
May I have a ride?

Participants: Sorry, horse, you start with an H.
You cannot come inside.

Leader: I'm a wasp, a wasp, a buzzing wasp.
May I have a ride?

Participants: Yes, wasp starts with a W.
Come on and ride inside.

Leader: I'm a lamb, a lamb, a little lamb.
May I have a ride?

Participants: Sorry, lamb, you start with an L.
You cannot come inside.

Leader: I'm the wind, the wind, the roaring wind,
May I have a ride?

Participants: Yes, wind starts with a W.
Come on and ride inside.

Leader: I'm a cat, a cat, a cute cuddly cat.
May I have a ride?

Participants: Sorry, cat, you start with a C.
You cannot come inside.

Leader: I'm the water, the water, the wet, wet water. May I have a ride?

Participants: Yes, water starts with a W. Come on and ride inside.

Leader: I'm a pig, a pig, a pretty, pink pig. May I have a ride?

Participants: Sorry, pig, you start with a P. You cannot come inside.

Leader: I'm a bird, a bird, a beautiful bird. May I have a ride?

Participants: Sorry, bird, you start with a B. You cannot come inside.

Leader: I'm a wall, a wall, a tall, tall wall. May I have a ride?

Participants: Yes, wall starts with a W. Come on and ride inside.

Leader: I'm a watch, a watch, a ticking watch. May I have a ride?

Participants: Yes, watch starts with a W. Come on and ride inside.

Leader: This is the W Wagon.

Participants: This is the W Wagon.

Leader: If you start with a W.

Participants: Welcome aboard!

W is for Weaving

Paper weaving is a mess-free and challenging craft. Older students and adults can create beautiful Op Art using the same basic technique. So many weaving words begin with the W sound!

Materials:
- copies of the warp and weft patterns for paper weaving. To save time, you may wish to duplicate the warp on a one color of paper and the weft on paper with a harmonizing hue.
- scissors
- glue sticks
- markers (if you duplicated both pages on white)
- a sample finished paper weaving
- a sample folded and cut warp
- sample weft strips (in a contrasting color)

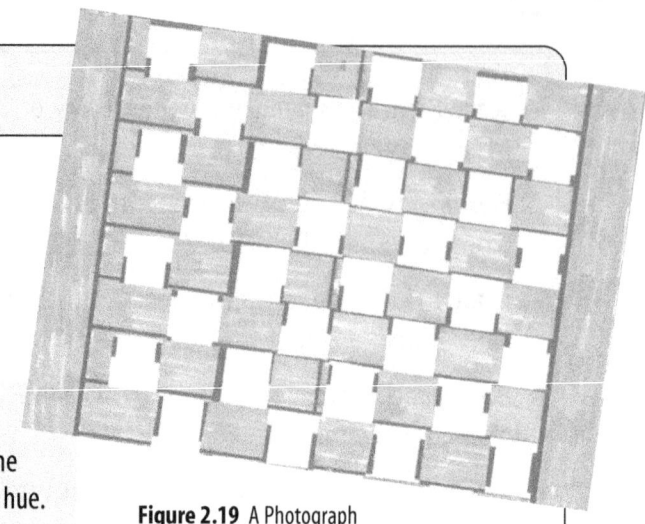

Figure 2.19 A Photograph of a Finished Paper Weaving Project

Procedure:
- Show students the sample weaving. Point out that it has two parts. Each part has a W name.
- Hold up the sample warp. Explain that it has strips attached to a frame at the top and the bottom.
- Hold up the weft strips. Explain that they will be woven over and under the strips in the warp.
- If you duplicated both pages on white copy paper, distribute the weft page, and encourage students to color them. They can color all of the strips one color, or they can fill them with rainbow hues.
- Next, distribute the warp page and scissors.
- Show students how to fold the paper along the marked center line. The cutting lines should be on the outside. Show them the heavy stopping lines at the top of each strip. Tell them not to cut beyond those lines. Remind them that the warp strips are attached at the top and the bottom.
- Demonstrate how to cut along each line, starting at the fold, and stopping at the heavy cross line. Put the warp aside.
- Show students how to cut along the lines to make the weft strips. This time, they can cut all the way across.
- Demonstrate how to weave the first weft strip over and under the strips in the warp. Explain that the strips will alternate. If the first strip started over, the second strip will start under.
- Push the second strip up beside the first one.
- Repeat to finish the weaving. Add a dot of stick glue to the end of each woven weft strip to make the piece stronger.

From the Studio:
Help students weave a placemat using two colors of construction paper. Simplify strip measuring. Give students cardboard templates to trace. Cutting the strips in advance is also a viable option.

Pattern for Paper Weaving Warp

fold
fold

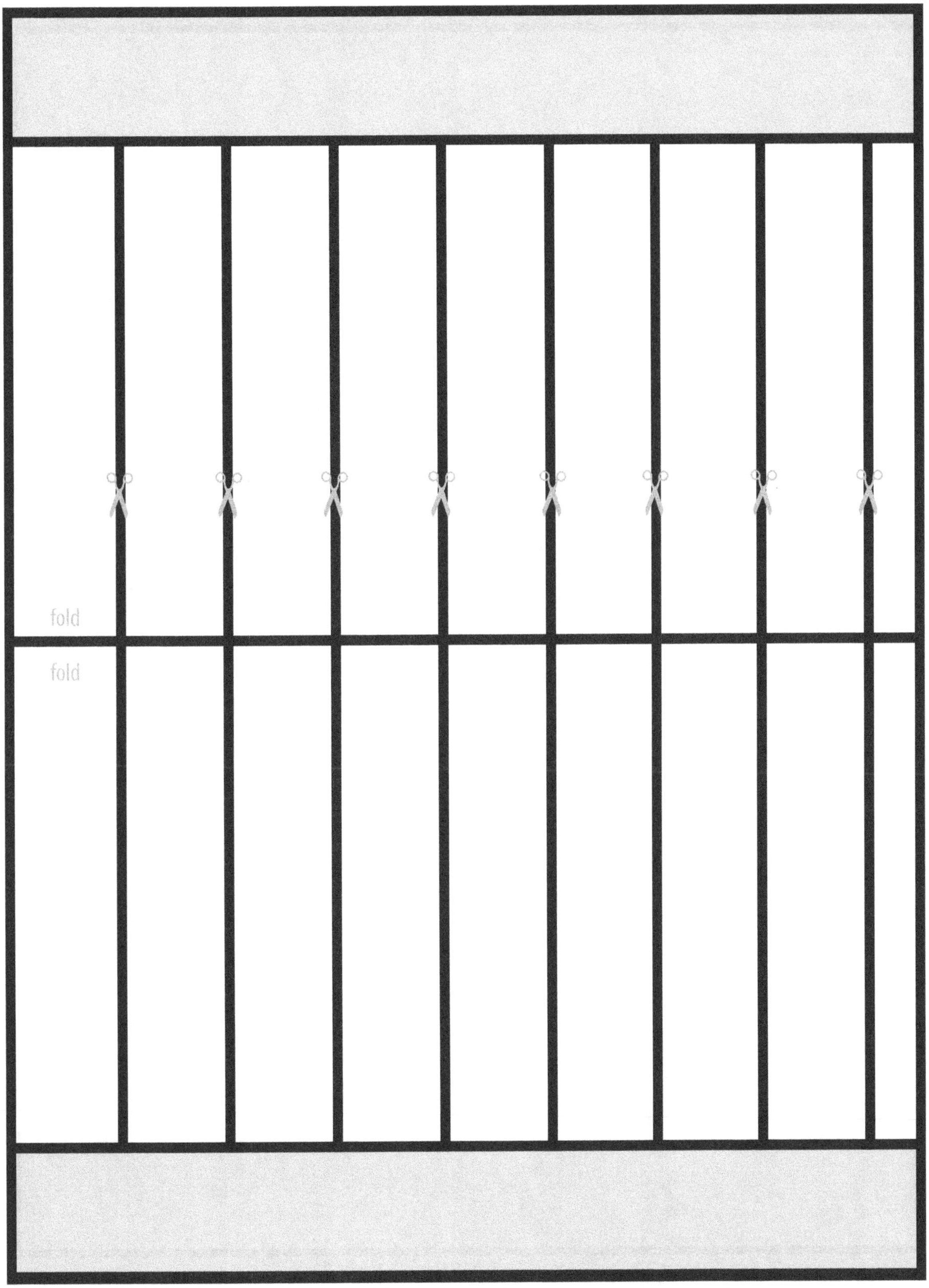

Figure 2.20 Pattern for Paper Weaving Warp

Pattern for Paper Weaving Warp

Pattern for Paper Weaving Weft

Figure 2.21 Pattern for Paper Weaving Weft

Unit 12: C

C IS FOR COLOR

Combine a study of basic primary and secondary colors with an introduction to the hard (K) sound of the letter C. Encourage students to say the first line of each stanza. Teach it to them before presenting the poem.

C is for Color

C is for color, and yellow is one:
Yellow lemon and yellow sun.
C is for color, and another is blue:
Summer sky and water, too.
C is for color. I like green:
Grass on a hill in a springtime scene.
C is for color. Red is bright:
Reflected signals on a rainy night.
C is for color. Purple is deep:
In purple haze, the mountains sleep.
C is for color. Orange is sweet:
Brilliant oranges are a winter treat.
C is for colors. I like them all:
Green in the summer; gold in the fall.
C is for colors. They make me sing:
White in the winter, pink in the spring.
C is for colors, soft or bright,
Without them, the world would be black and white.

C is for Color Wheel

Here's an easy, pretty project that introduces participants to color theory. The color wheel teaches sequence and relationships.

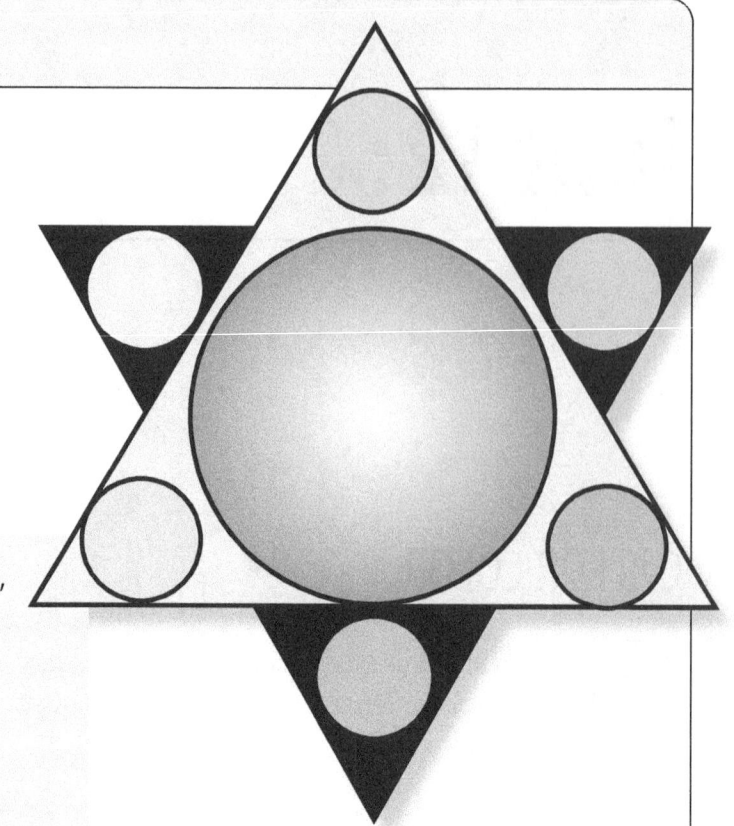

Materials:
- One sheet each of Red, yellow, blue, orange, green, and purple construction paper
- copies of A Color Wheel Pattern
- markers or crayons
- sample color wheel

Procedure:

- Review the hard C sound. Encourage students to name other words that begin with the same sound as color. Do not worry about spelling (i.e. words that really begin with K) for the purpose of this session.

- Call for three volunteers. Give each one a sheet representing a primary color. Explain that these colors are important because they can be mixed to make all of the other colors.

- Have the three volunteers stand facing the group, holding up their colors.

- Encourage participants to name each color in turn.

- Select another volunteer. Give him the sheet of orange paper.

- Invite group members to name the new color.

- Ask if anybody can guess which two colors could be mixed together to make orange.

- Have the volunteer stand between red and yellow. Repeat these steps with green and purple.

- Show color wheel sample. Distribute copies of the page and crayons.

- Review the names and placements of the colors before students color the circles.

From the Studio:

Explore primary and secondary colors with watercolor. Drip red, yellow, and blue watercolor on wet paper and watch the hues mix on the page.

Color Wheel Pattern

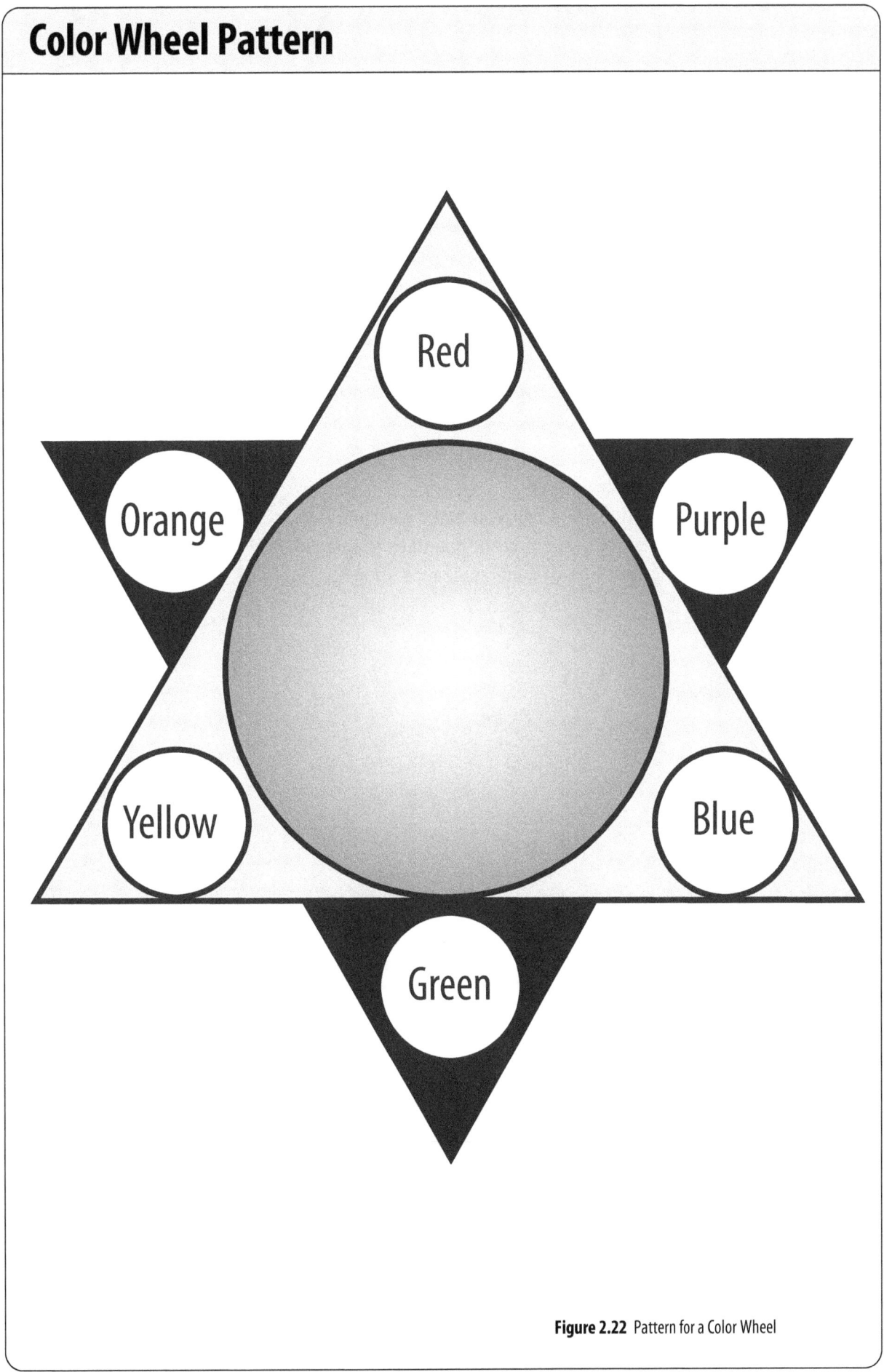

Figure 2.22 Pattern for a Color Wheel

Unit 13: G

GOGGLES

Learn or review the hard G sound as you make a virtual deep sea dive with this verse. Motions are suggested, but they are not mandatory. Instead, you might choose to have the group repeat the first line of each stanza, as shown.

Section 2: Consonants

G is for Goggles

Leader: G is for goggles.
(Make goggles by touching the tip of each thumb to the tip of each forefinger.)

Participants: G is for goggles.
Put them on.
(Repeat this pattern with each verse, if not doing the motions.)
(Hold the finger goggles in front of your eyes.)

Take a deep breath, and dive.
(Hold your nose, take a deep breath, and close your eyes.)

G for green: Green kelp waving all around.
(Hold both arms over your head and wave them slowly from side to side, like seaweed in the water.)

G for graceful: Graceful dolphins
Gliding by.
(Put both palms together in front of you. You now have a dolphin's body. Move it away from you and toward the audience with a swimming motion or a zooming motion, whichever you prefer.)

G is for ghostly: Ghostly jellyfish
Hovering near.
(Hold your arms out in front of you so that your palms face down and your fingers dangle down. That is a jellyfish. Move your fingers like the creature's appendages. It's hovering, so it doesn't have to move around.)

G is for glistening: Glistening fish
Swimming in schools.
(Cup each hand slightly. Hold each one sideways and press your thumb tightly to the top of the "fish." Move both hands in the same direction like two fish swimming in a school, then make them change direction.)

G is for gloomy: Gloomy deeps
Lying below.
(Shade your eyes with your hand and peer downward)

G is for glowing: The glowing surface
Beckons us up.
(Hold your arms overhead with both palms facing outward. Move your hands down while looking upward, as if swimming up to the surface.)

Take off your goggles: (Hold the goggles up, and then lower them.)
Breathe the fresh air. (Take a deep breath.)
Climb in the boat.

G is for golden: A golden sunset (Point toward the audience.)
Leads us home. (Fold your hands in your lap.)

A Goofy Goggles Craft

Figure 2.23 A Photograph of the Finished Goggles Project.

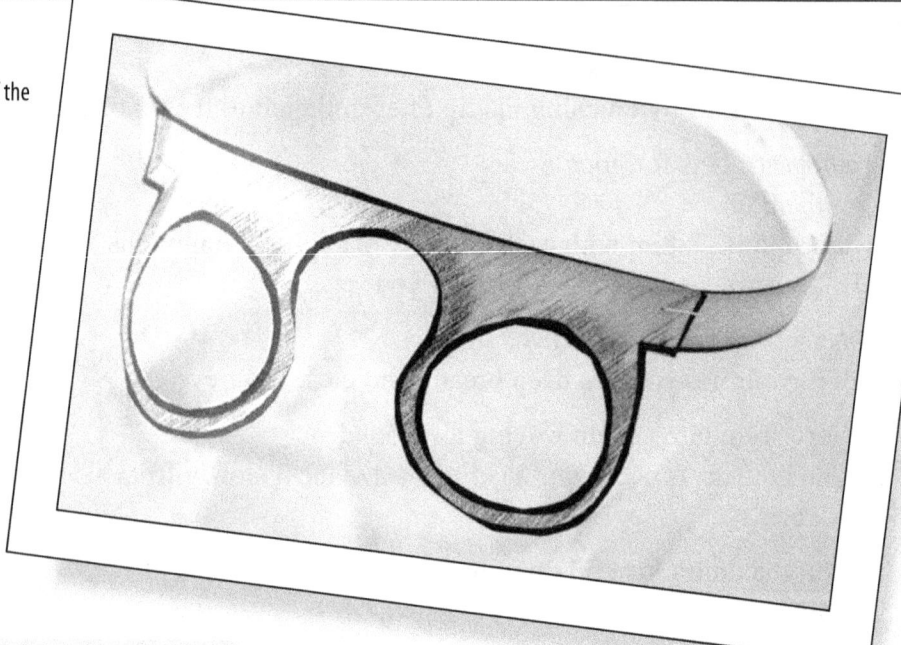

Materials:
- copies of A Goggles Pattern
- markers
- scissors
- a sample pair of goggles
- clear tape, glue, or staples and a stapler

Hints:
Can't think of examples?
A list of words for each letter is included at the end of this book.

Procedure:
- Review the hard G sound. Encourage students to name other hard G words.
- Show students the sample goggles.
- Cut out along the outside edges of the goggles.
- Demonstrate how to fold and cut the center of each "glass" of the goggles. A fold line is marked on the pattern.
- Help students tape, glue or staple a strip of headband to each side of the goggles. This will not be long enough. Staple the long strip to either side. Then try on the band to find the right spot to staple the ends together. The headband should be easy to put on and take off.
- You may wish to choose a child who is average sized and fit the headband in advance, then mark the spot for the final staple before reproducing the page for the group.

From the Studio:
Expand the underwater theme by encouraging students to draw goldfish with crayons. Tell them to color the fish in, pressing hard. Then, instruct them to paint over the page with blue watercolor.

A Goggles Pattern Page

At Home
Put on your goggles. Look for something that begins with G.

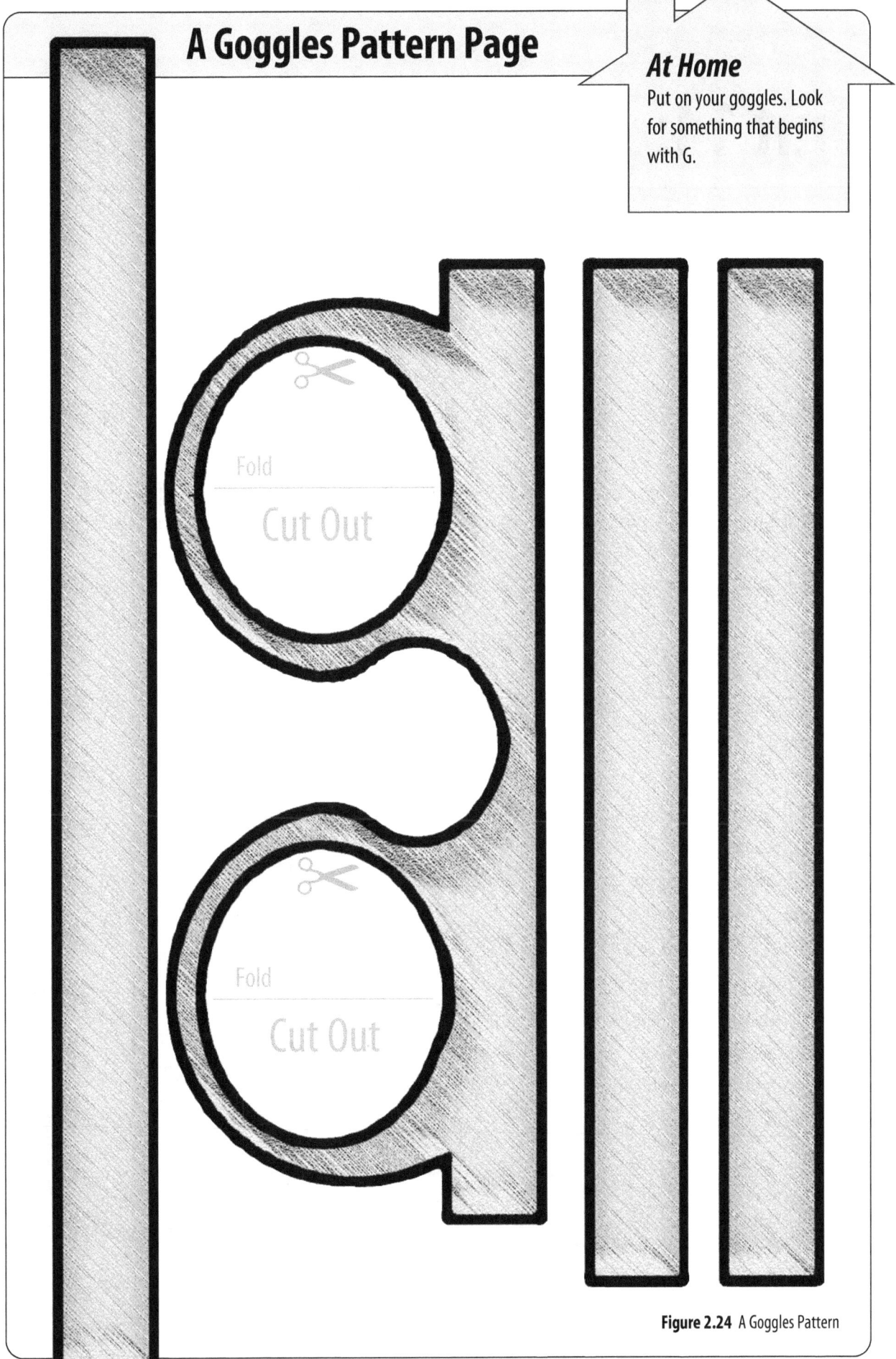

Figure 2.24 A Goggles Pattern

ABC, Follow Me! Phonics Rhymes and Crafts, Grades K-1

Unit 14: J

JEWELS

Introduce the letter J by placing it on a flannel board. Show a large fake jewel. Explain that the word jewel begins with a J. Ask for other words that begin with a J. Responses might include juice, jam, and jar.

J is for Jewelry

My mom wears chains and beads.
She sometimes wears a pin.
On rainy days she lets us take
The box she puts them in.
She has a golden jaguar,
A blue jewel in a ring,
She has a silver bracelet
And pink pearls on a string.
What a hoard of treasures
For pirate kids to steal!
They gleam and they glitter,
But none of them is real.

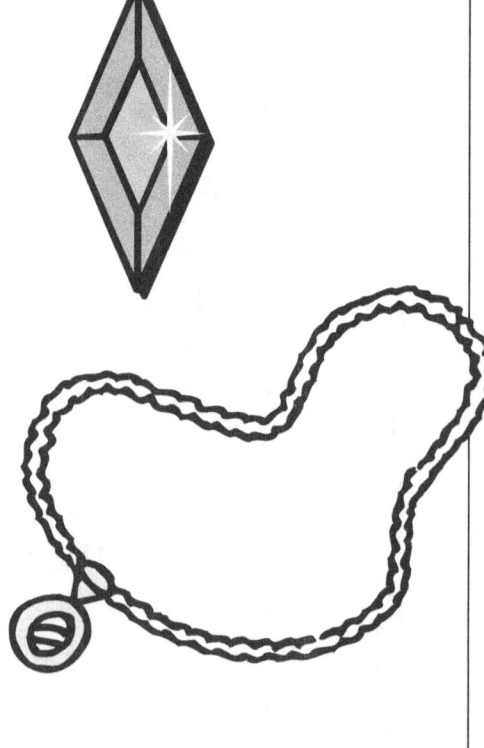

J is for Jewelry

Figure 2.25 A Photograph of Finished Paper Bracelets

Procedure:

- Remind students that the word jewelry begins with a J. A bracelet is one kind of jewelry, and that is what they are going to be making. Ask students to describe pieces of jewelry they have seen.
- Show the sample bracelet.
- Demonstrate each step just before students do it.
- Color the bracelet strips with markers.
- Glue the ends together to make loops.
- The finished bracelets should be loose enough to slip on and off easily.

Materials:
- copies of A Pattern for a J Bracelet
- markers
- scissors
- glue sticks
- finished sample J bracelet

From the Studio:
Other jewelry projects include papier mache or craft clay pendants, and paperclip chain bracelets. Consult books such as *Step-By-Step Crafts for Children* by the Editors of Kingfisher to find directions for these and other handmade jewelry projects.

Patterns for J Bracelets

At Home
Use the patterns and colored markers or colored pencils to make more paper jewelry. To make your bracelets last longer, cover them with clear tape.

Figure 2.25 Patterns for J Bracelets

Section 2: Consonants

Unit 15: R

RATTLE, ROAR, AND RUMBLE

Long before they learn the word onomatopoeia, children are playing with imitative sounds. Many languages have an equivalent of "Old McDonald's Farm." Here's a sound song to teach or review the letter R. Before presenting the poem, write the letter Rr on the board, place it on the flannel board, or invite a volunteer to hold up a prepared Rr placard. The last verse is a memory challenge. Pause and encourage participants to fill in the correct sound words, in the correct sequence, from previous verses.

R is for Rattle

The wind is blowing. The gate is rattling.
(Put closed hands in front of you and pretend to rattle a gate.)

R is for rattling, rattling, rattling;

R is for rattling.

The lion is waking. Now he is roaring.
(Pretend to roar.)

R is for roaring, roaring, roaring;

R is for roaring.

Lightning is striking. Thunder is rumbling.
(Roll hands, as in "This Old Man")

R is for rumbling, rumbling, rumbling;

R is for rumbling.

It's three o'clock. Tower bells are ringing.
(pull on a bell rope)

R is for ringing, ringing, ringing;

R is for ringing.
(Do all actions.)

R is for gates rattling. R is for lions roaring, and gates rattling.

R is for thunder rumbling, lions roaring, and gates rattling.

R is for bells ringing, thunder rumbling, lions roaring, and gates rattling.

Rattling, roaring, rumbling, ringing; what a noisy letter!

OR

Assign a volunteer to perform each action
and tell participants to point to the right performer
at each point in the verse.

R is for Rattle: A Water Bottle Rattle

Figure 2.27 Photograph of a Finished Bottle Rattle

Procedure:

- Show students the sample rattle.
- Demonstrate how to put the beans into the bottle. More beans will make a different sound than fewer.
- Put the lid on the bottle.
- Color the bottle label.
- Cut out the label and glue it in place on the bottle. It will be a cylindrical sleeve.

Materials:

- empty, dry water bottles with screw-top lids
- dried beans
- copies of the label pattern
- finished water bottle rattle sample
- scissors
- markers
- glue

From the Studio:

Other R-inspired art projects include relief prints (string prints or foam block prints) and rubbings.

A Label for a Water Bottle Rattle

Figure 2.28 A Label for a Water Bottle Rattle

Unit 16: P

PEOPLE, PEOPLE, PEOPLE

Introduce or review the sound of the letter P with this verse. Before presenting the rhyme, write the letter Pp on the board or on lined chart paper. Explain that P makes the sound heard at the beginning of people. Encourage participants to repeat the word after you. Then say you want them to say people every time you point to them. Practice with a few sentences such as the following:

- Boys and girls are (Point to the group, and they should say people.)
- Men and women are
- Teachers and students are
- Friends and family are

P is for People

P is for people, for boys and girls,
People with straight hair, people with curls.
P is for people with blue eyes and brown,
People that smile and people that frown.
P is for people, the short and the tall,
Tots in the park and teens at the mall.
P is for people, the young and the old,
The shy and quiet, the loud and bold.
People is for people in cars, planes, or boats.
P is for people in shorts, sweats, or coats.
P is for people, strong, smart, and free.
P is for people like you and like me.

Folded Paper People

This traditional craft has fascinated children for generations. It is also a great introduction to the power of symmetry and repetition. The printed pattern makes the first set of paper people easy. After they have finished the sample, participants may enjoy seeing how to cut longer strings of paper people from newspaper. Start with a strip, and make accordion folds. The more folds you make, the more people there will be in your string. Next, cut out half a girl or boy. Just be sure to cut off across the fold in two places (the hands and feet) so your people will be joined together. (See the boy in the example.)

Procedure:

- Remind students that the word people begins with a P. Ask them to name some of their favorite people. While you are talking, fold and cut the sample people. Then, with a flourish, unfold them.
- You are going to create an accordion fold. Fold the center first, keeping the guidelines on the outside. Then, fold each outside edge toward the folded edge.
- Tell participants that they will be learning how to do this paper people trick.
- Distribute the materials.
- Instruct participants to perform each step with you.
- Encourage students to add clothes, hair, and features to their finished paper people.

Materials:
- copies of A Pattern for Folded Paper People
- scissors
- markers
- sample of finished folded paper people
- sticks

From the Studio:
Other P-inspired projects include paper bag puppets, pulled string paintings, pencil drawings, and printmaking.

Pattern for Folded Paper People

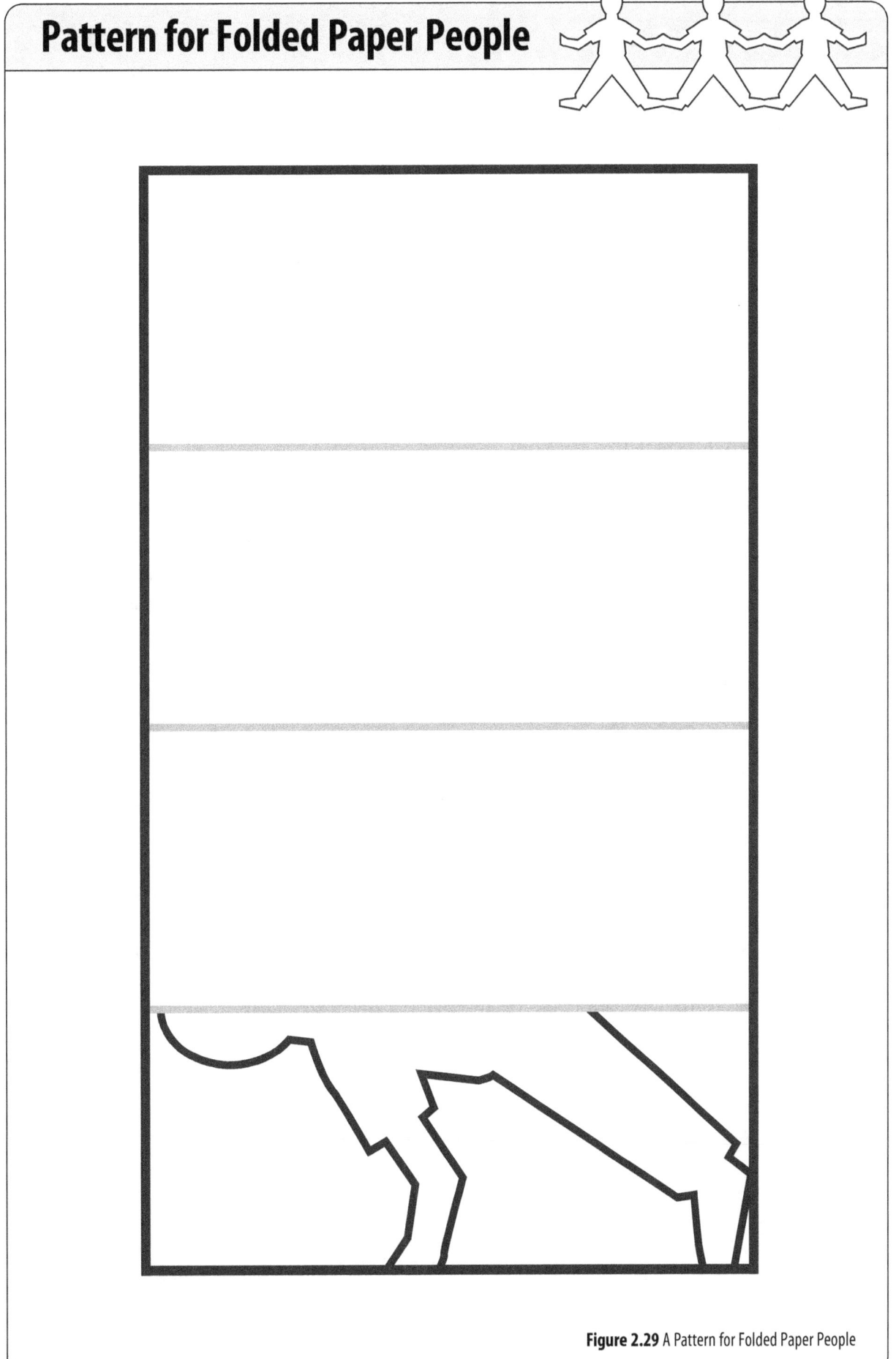

Figure 2.29 A Pattern for Folded Paper People

ABC, Follow Me! Phonics Rhymes and Crafts, Grades K–1

Unit 17: V

V IS FOR VEGETABLE

Introduce or review the sound of the letter V with this cumulative verse. Begin by writing a letter V on the board or in the middle of a sheet of chart paper. Say that it stands for the sound heard at the beginning of the word valley. Add a slanted line to either side of the V to change it into two mountain peaks with a valley between them. If desired, use squiggly lines near the top of each peak to indicate snow.

If you have a flannel board, patterns for the items mentioned in the verse are included. Add the details with black permanent marker. Add a new vegetable with each verse and point to the previous ones to help students remember what comes next in the cumulative pattern.

Before beginning, explain that when you rub your tummy they should repeat the last line you said, and then add V is for Vegetables. Yum! Read the first verse and give participants a chance to respond. Then, move on to the second verse. Tell them that this time when you rub your tummy, they will repeat A sweet, orange carrot, and then they will add the last line from the new verse. Read the second stanza and help them respond. The flannel board figures will help. Point to the carrot and then to the peapod.

Hints:
Instead of using the flannel board, you may wish to make the patterns into a transparency and use the overhead projector, or scan them into the computer to create a PowerPoint presentation.

In a Very Green Valley

V is for vegetables
in a very green valley, touched by a very bright sun.
Name a vegetable that's growing. A sweet, orange carrot is one.
(Rub your tummy and encourage students to respond as follows:)
A sweet, orange carrot;
V is for vegetables. Yum!

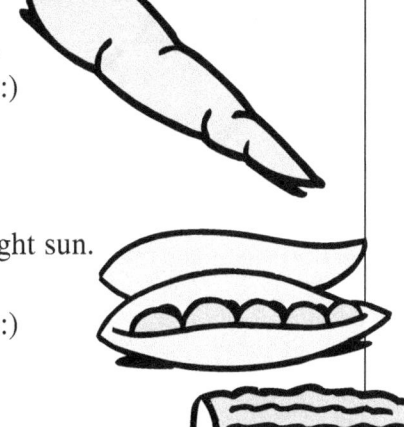

V is for vegetables in a very green valley, touched by a very bright sun.
Name a vegetable that's growing. A crisp, green peapod is one.
(Rub your tummy and encourage students to respond as follows:)
A sweet, orange carrot; a crisp, green peapod;
V is for vegetables. Yum!

V is for vegetables in a very green valley, touched by a very bright sun.
Name a vegetable that's growing. A long, striped zucchini is one.
(Rub your tummy and encourage students to respond as follows:)
A sweet, orange carrot; a crisp, green peapod; a long, striped zucchini;
V is for vegetables. Yum!

V is for vegetables in a very green valley, touched by a very bright sun.
Name a vegetable that's growing. Corn on the cob is one.
(Rub your tummy and encourage students to respond as follows:)
A sweet, orange carrot; a crisp, green peapod; a long, striped zucchini;
Corn on the cob;
V is for vegetables. Yum!

V is for vegetables in a very green valley, touched by a very bright sun.
Name a vegetable that's growing. A round head of lettuce is one.
(Rub your tummy and encourage students to respond as follows:)
A sweet, orange carrot; a crisp, green peapod; a long, striped zucchini;
Corn on the cob; a round head of lettuce;
V is for vegetables. Yum!

V is for vegetables in a very green valley, touched by a very bright sun.
Name a vegetable that's growing. A big, orange pumpkin is one.
(Rub your tummy and encourage students to respond as follows:)
A sweet, orange carrot; a crisp, green peapod;
A long, striped zucchini; corn on the cob; a round head of lettuce;
A big, orange pumpkin;
V is for vegetables. Yum!

Flannel Board Patterns for V is for Vegetables

At Home
Color the vegetables. Cut them out. Glue your favorite vegetable to a magnet and put it on the refrigerator door.

Figure 2.30 Vegetable Flannel Board Patterns

V is for Vegetable Print

Prints are easy and great fun. Vegetable prints are great for beginners, and, of course, the word vegetable begins with a V.

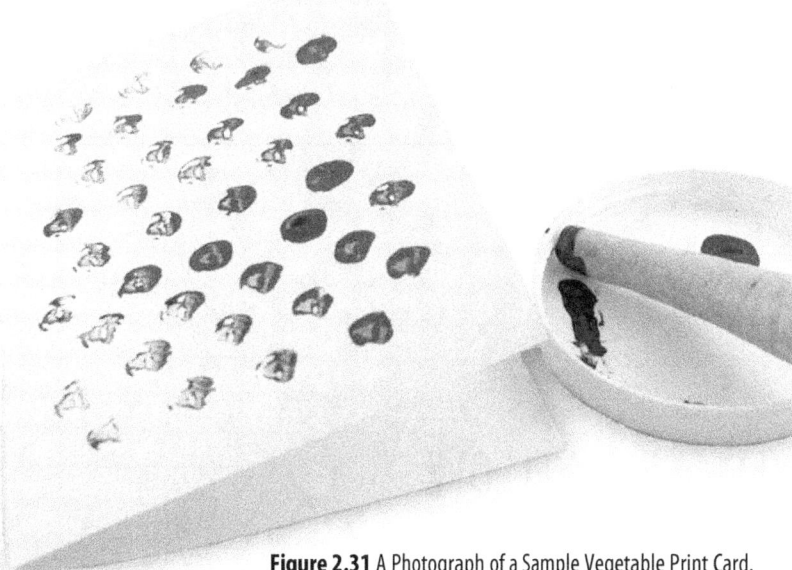

Figure 2.31 A Photograph of a Sample Vegetable Print Card.

Materials:
- carrots sliced into two inch sections to make round printing "blocks"
- stamp pads with water-soluble ink or tempera-soaked paper towels on foam snack plates
- paper

From the Studio:
Expand this project by making prints with other fruits and vegetables. Potatoes work well. So do large sliced zucchini, the kind with big seeds. Cut softer vegetables in advance and place sliced ends on paper towels to absorb excess moisture. In the library, use the flannel board pattern sheet as a coloring page. Encourage students to draw a vegetable monster or superhero on the back of the page. For example, they might draw the Corn Monster with twenty eyes or Carrot Man with a green cape.

Procedure:
- Remind students that the word vegetable begins with a V. Encourage participants to name as many other V words as possible.
- Explain that you will be making prints with one kind of vegetable, a carrot. Encourage them to predict what shape the carrot will make when it is printed.
- Demonstrate how to create a repeating pattern by printing the carrot.
- Distribute materials.
- Demonstrate how to fold the paper in half to create a greeting card.
- Encourage students to create a printed design on the front of the card. Use colors appropriate to the season.

Unit 18: Y

YELL, YELL, YELLOW

Here's a rowdy salute to the letter Y and the color yellow. Before sharing the poem, introduce the letter Y. Then present some riddles to elicit Y words. When students are familiar with the sound, teach them the refrain, "yell, yell, yellow!" Say the phrase at the exact volume you would like the group to use.

Hints:
Kids love to jump around and make noise, but sometimes over-stimulation can be a problem. If yelling isn't appropriate for your setting, try whispering. As performers know, a certain amount of tension between meaning and mode of delivery can be fun.

Y Riddles

What is the opposite of "no?"

What has twelve months?

What do you do when you are tired? (demonstrate a yawn)

What does your grandma use when she knits?

What is the yellow part of an egg?

What was the day before today?

Section 2: Consonants

Yell, Yell, Yellow!

Yellow slickers, yellow lemons;
yell, yell, yellow!
Yellow bananas, yellow lights;
yell, yell, yellow!
Yellow sun, yellow pencils;
yell, yell, yellow!
Yellow shirt, yellow lines;
yell, yell, yellow!
Yellow leaves, yellow cheese;
yell, yell, yellow!
Yellow butter, yellow trees;
yell, yell, yellow!
Yellow bus, yellow chalk;
yell, yell, yellow!
Yellow squash, yellow bird;
yell, yell, yellow!
Yellow is a noisy word.
Yell, yell, yellow!

Y is for Yellow Leaves: A Sponge Print Project

Materials:
- a finished sponge-printed leaf picture
- household sponges cut into squares
- yellow paper
- large, sturdy leaves (sycamore or maple)
- tempera paint on foam plates (any color except yellow)
- trash bags and paper towels or sponges for cleanup

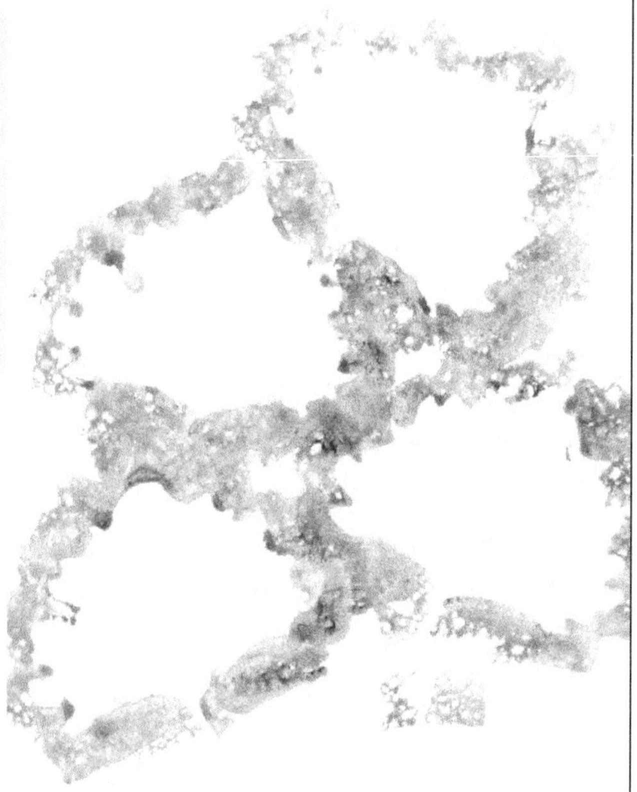

Figure 2.32 A Scan of a Sponge-Printed Leaf

Procedure:
- Review the letter Y. Encourage participants to share words that begin with Y.
- Ask what happens to leaves in the fall. Explain that they will be making yellow leaves.
- Show the finished sample.
- Put a leaf on a yellow sheet of paper.
- Dip the end of a sponge square into the paint, then, holding the leaf with one hand, dab around the outside of it with the paint.
- When the sponge square starts to run out of paint, dip it again.
- Remove the leaf.
- Distribute materials.
- Assist students as they work.

From the Studio:

Although this is a relatively neat painting project, tempera is always messy. In the library, invite students to create an autumn scene using The Letter Y, a Tree Trunk Pattern.

Figure 2.33 A Scan of a Finished Letter Y Tree Picture

Section 2: Consonants

Letter Y: A Tree Trunk Pattern

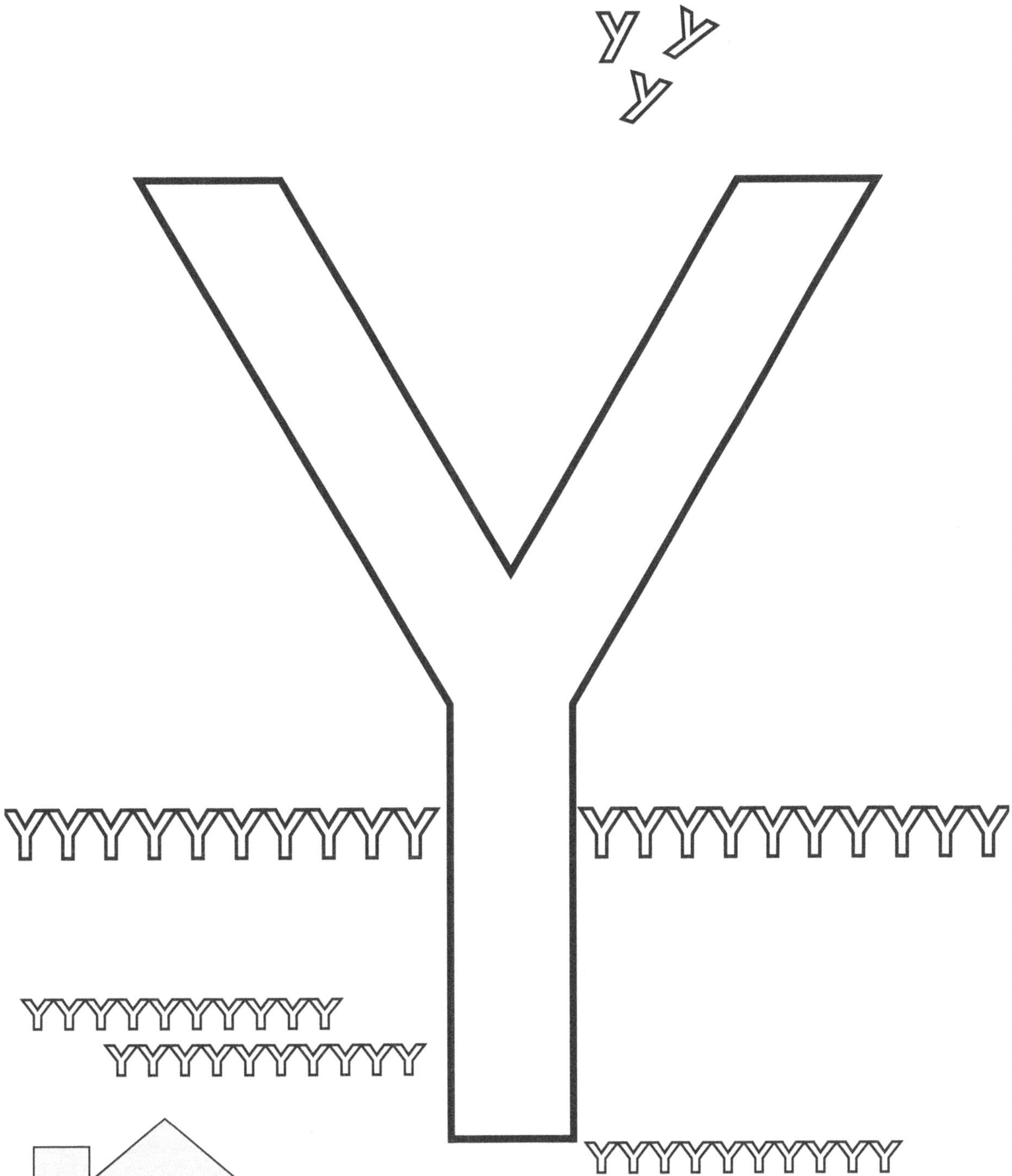

At Home
On this page, Y is a tree trunk. It is also grass and a fence. Add leaves and colors to finish the picture. Draw some children jumping in a pile of leaves.

Figure 2.34 A Letter Y Tree Trunk Pattern

Letter Y: A Tree Trunk Pattern

ABC, Follow Me! Phonics Rhymes and Crafts, Grades K–1

Unit 19: Z

ZOOM, ZING, ZONE, ZAP!

Introduce the letter Z by writing it on the board or by placing it on a flannel board. Encourage children to buzz like bees. Then, invite them to repeat some Z words after you, buzzing at the beginning of each.

Z Words
zebra, zap, zigzag, zipper, zoo, zone, zoom, zero

Hints: When introducing an action verse, start very slowly. Give participants time to watch and imitate words or movements.

Zoom, Zing, Zone, Zap!

First, hold your hands up.
(Hold up your palms facing the audience)

Give your lap a slap. (Slap your thighs once)

Roll and roll and roll and roll,
(Roll your hands over each other as if doing "This Old Man")

And then you can clap.
(Clap once) Zoom, zing, zone, zap!

Up, slap, roll, clap!
(Hands up, slap thighs, roll hands, clap)

Zoom, zing, zone, zap! Up, slap, roll, clap!
(Hands up, slap thighs, roll hands, clap)

Zooming down the rollercoaster,

Hands in the air, feel the wind against your face.

At the county fair.

Zoom, zing, zone, zap! Up, slap, roll, clap!
(Hands up, slap thighs, roll hands, clap)

Zoom, zing, zone, zap! Up, slap, roll, clap!
(Hands up, slap thighs, roll hands, clap)

Zing! (Slap your knees) Did I get you?

On the yard with friends, someone tells a tricky joke and laughs when it ends.

Zoom, zing, zone, zap! Up, slap, roll, clap!
(Hands up, slap thighs, roll hands, clap)

Zoom, zing, zone, zap! Up, slap, roll, clap!
(Hands up, slap thighs, roll hands, clap)

Rolling along slowly, you are not alone.

You are driving a yellow bus in a safety zone.

Zoom, zing, zone, zap! Up, slap, roll, clap!
(Hands up, slap thighs, roll hands, clap)

Zoom, zing, zone, zap! Up, slap, roll, clap!
(Hands up, slap thighs, roll hands, clap)

Zzz: Do you hear that? It woke me from my nap.

I think it's a mosquito. I see it, now, zap! (clap)

Zoom, zing, zone, zap! Up, slap, roll, clap!
(Hands up, slap thighs, roll hands, clap)

Zoom, zing, zone, zap! Up, slap, roll, clap!
(Hands up, slap thighs, roll hands, clap)

Z is for Zigzag: An Accordion Book

Here's a simple style of bookbinding that older artists develop into beautiful albums and portfolios.

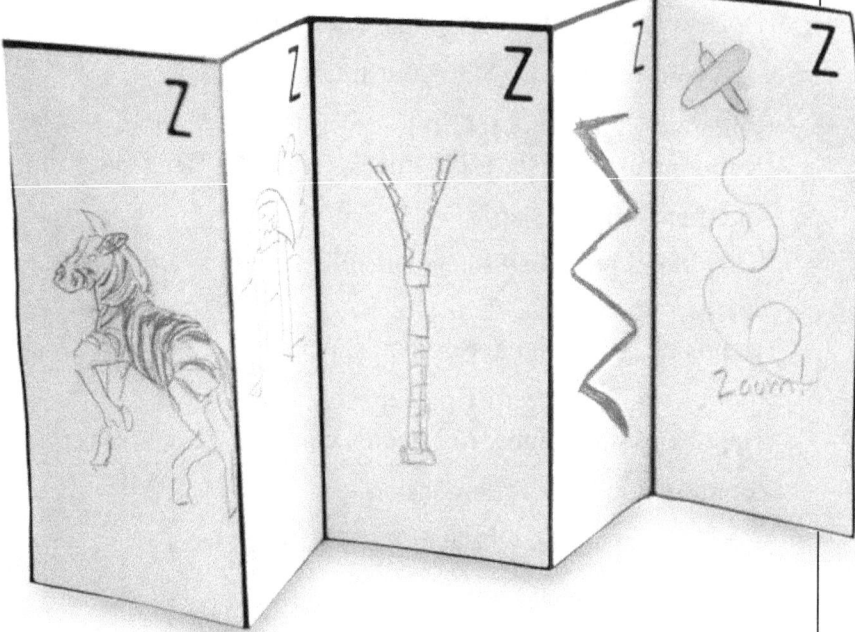

Figure 2.35 Photograph of a Finished Zigzag Book

Materials:
- copies of A Pattern for a Letter Z Accordion Book
- a finished accordion book made from the pattern
- scissors
- crayons or markers

From the Studio:
Expand on this project by making Zigzag books for other letters, or for numbers. The same folding technique may be used to create fans.

Procedure:
- Review the sound of Z and some Z words. (See the boxed list on the Zoom, Zing, Zone, Zap! page.)
- Show participants the sample book. Point out that there is a picture on each page.
- Demonstrate how to cut out the book and fold it on the lines.
- Distribute materials.

Pattern for a Letter Z Accordion Book

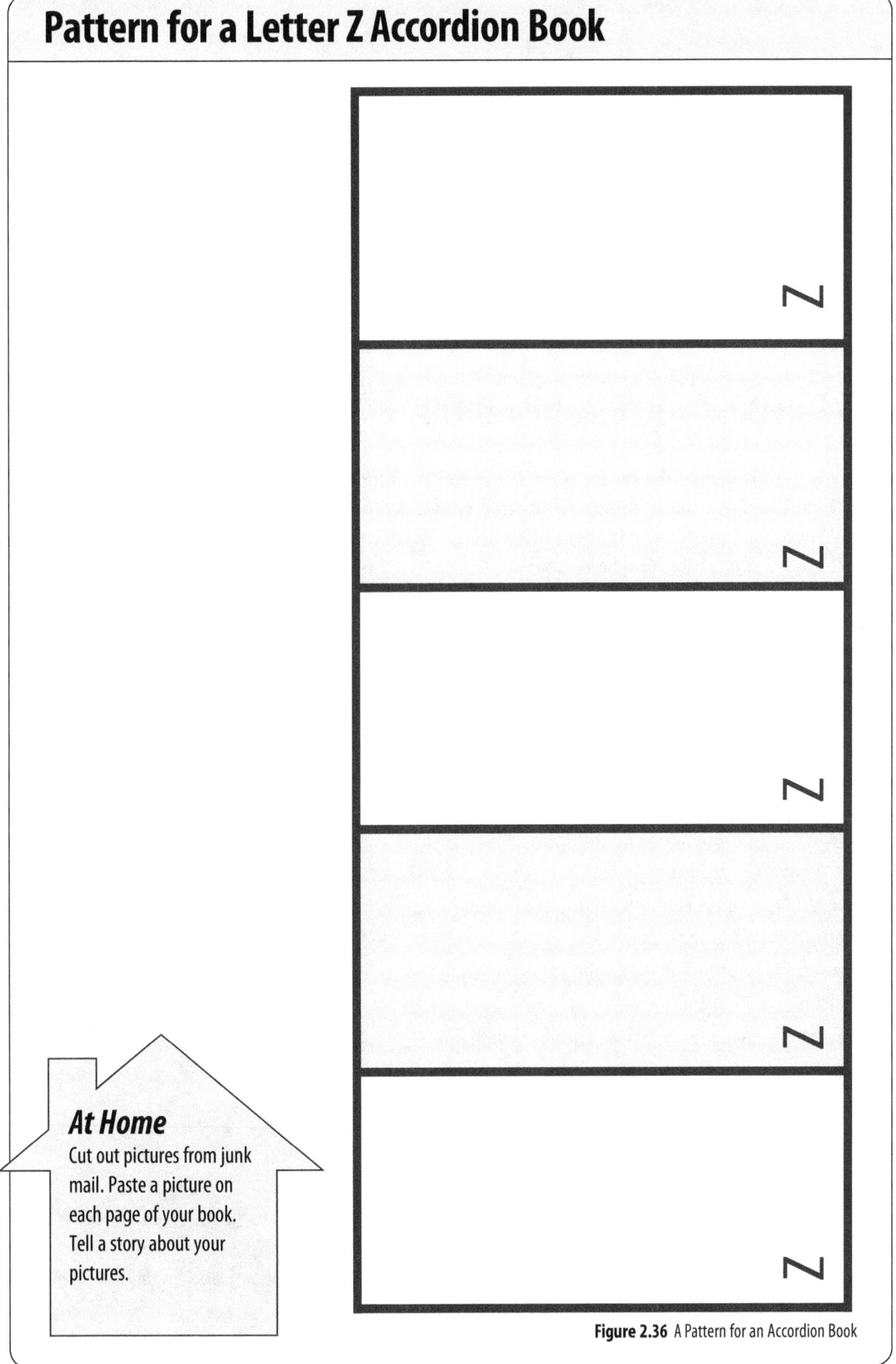

At Home
Cut out pictures from junk mail. Paste a picture on each page of your book. Tell a story about your pictures.

Figure 2.36 A Pattern for an Accordion Book

Pattern for a Letter Z Accordion Book

Unit 20: Q

Q IS FOR QUILT, QUIET, AND QUICK!

Before introducing the poem, write the letter Q on the board and use clues to elicit words that start with Q. Share a picture book with many Q words, such as *Quick, Quack, Quick* by Marsha Arnold.

After students have mastered the letter, introduce the poem. Students should join in on the second line of each stanza. Help them until they understand the pattern. Emphasize the Q word with your voice.

Q Cues
The opposite of slow is (quick).
The opposite of noisy is (quiet).
The opposite of answer is (question).
The opposite of start is (quit).
Not a king, but a (queen).

Q is for Quilt

Leader: My grandma has an old quilt on her bed.
Participants: Q is for quilt.
Leader: Her house is quiet when I come home.
Participants: Q is for quiet.
Leader: Her needle is quick when she sews.
Participants: Q is for quick.
Leader: She asks me questions about my day.
Participants: Q is for questions.
Leader: She gives me some quarters for the store.
Participants: Q is for quarters.
Leader: We walk to the corner and see some quail.
Participants: Q is for quail.
Leader: My grandma has an old quilt on her bed.
Participants: Q is for quilt.
Leader: And she is making a new one for me.

Section 2: Consonants

Q is for Quilt: A Quilt Square Project

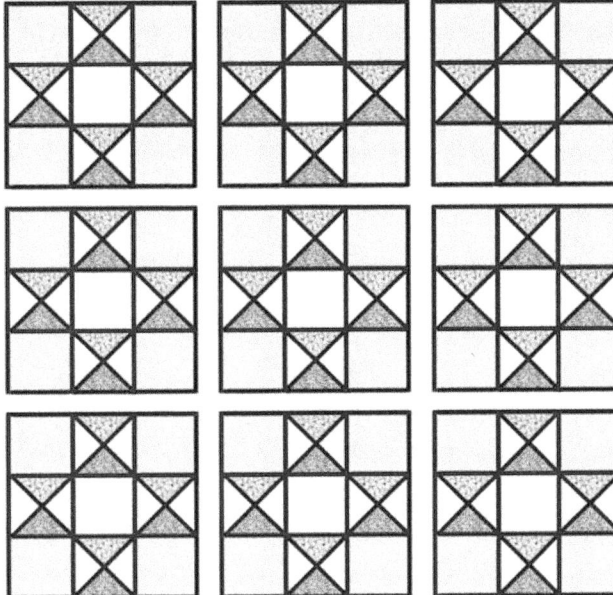

Figure 2.37 A Scan of the Finished Quilt Squares

Materials:
- copies of A Pattern for Two Quilt Squares
- markers or crayons
- scissors (optional)
- a picture book about quilting
- a sample of a finished quilt pattern page
- (If desired, make a sample of several squares pasted together on a larger page to form a pattern.)

From the Studio:
Require all students in the group to use the same three or four colors, and to follow the pattern closely. When the blocks are completed, arrange them on a sheet of mural paper to form a pattern and glue them in place for a classroom or hall display.

Procedure:
- Review the form and sound of the letter Q.
- If there is time, share a book about quilts like *Patchwork Island* by Karla Kushkin or *My Grandmother's Patchwork Quilt* by Janet Bolton.
- Show participants the finished sample.
- Demonstrate how to color the squares.
- Notice that there are four different textures or tones on each square.
- Use the same color to fill in spaces that have the same texture or tone. One square will use three colors; the other will use four.
- Distribute materials.
- Help students complete the project.

Pattern for Two Quilt Squares

At Home
On the back of this page, draw a bed with a quilt on it. Then draw the wall behind it. Put a window in the wall. Put curtains on the window. Draw yourself in the room.

Figure 2.38 Pattern for Two Quilt Squares

Unit 21: X

X is the End of Box

This action rhyme introduces or reviews the sound of X, along with a number of basic words. Begin by writing X on the board. Explain that it represents the sound heard at the end of the word box. Then, practice the following pattern with the group: Clap, clap, clap, slap, slap. Instead of clapping, students may hold up word cards. There are nine X word cards on the next page.

B-O-X Spells Box

B (Clap) O (Clap) X (Clap)
spells (slap lap) box (slap lap)
X (cross arms in front of you to form an X)
F-O-X spells fox.
X (cross arms in front of you to form an X)
M-A-X spells Max.
X (cross arms in front of you to form an X)
W-A-X spells Wax.
X (cross arms in front of you to form an X)
F-I-X spells Fix.
X (cross arms in front of you to form an X)
M-I-X spells Mix.
X (cross arms in front of you to form an X)
Box, fox, max, wax, fix, mix

X Ending Cards

At Home
Draw six beautiful gift boxes. Imagine that each box contains something you have wished for. Tell someone what is inside one of the boxes.

box	fox	ax
wax	six	fix
mix	tux	Max

Figure 2.39 Cards for Words Ending with X

Glowing X's: A Wax Resist Project

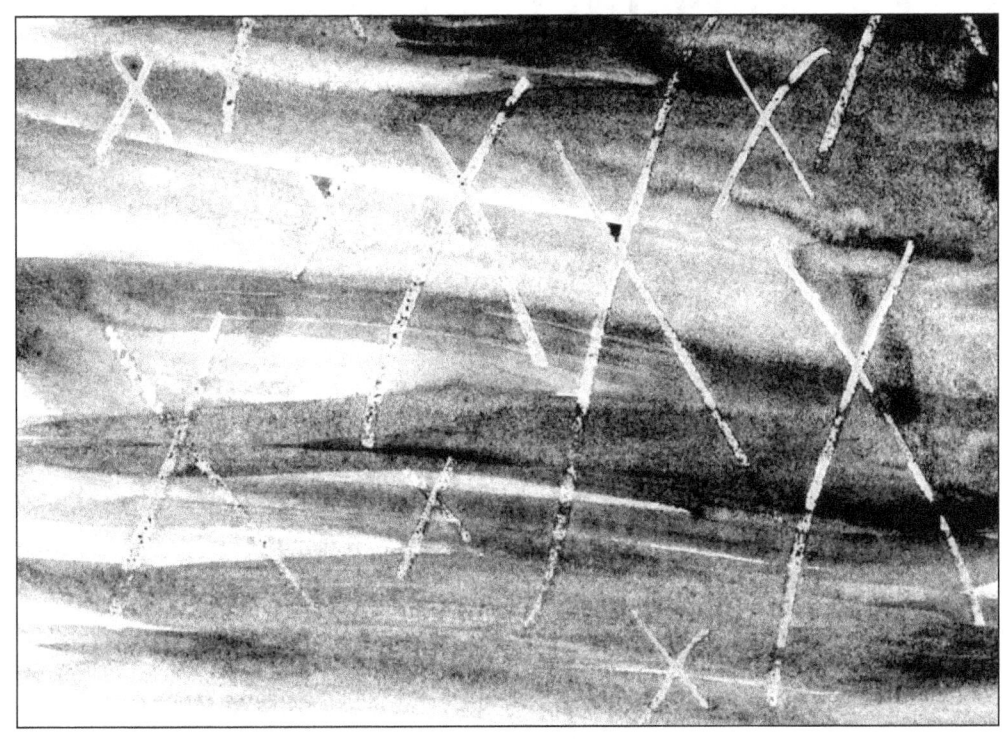

Figure 2.40 Scan of a Wax Resist Project

Procedure:

- Show the sample artwork.
- Draw several X's with light-colored crayons. Yellow, pink, or white work well. Then, paint over the letters with black watercolor. The wax in the crayons will resist the water in the paint, but the color will soak into the paper, leaving glowing lines against a dark background. Fluorescent crayons will intensify the effect. For a very magical experience, draw with white emergency candles (available at hardware stores) on white paper. The letters will be invisible until the paint is applied.

Materials:

- sample wax resist picture
- paper
- crayons or white candles
- black watercolor
- water in containers
- brushes

From the Studio:

In the library, distribute paper and invite students to draw a large X. The crossbars should stretch from corner to corner of the page. Encourage students to color the top and bottom sections one color, and the two sides a different color.

Unit 22: Medial Consonants

MIDDLE RIDDLES

Sometimes consonants are in the middle or at the end of a word. These silly riddles are designed to help children hear medial consonants. If children do not guess the missing word, give them the beginning sound. For example, you might say "a funny bu-" or "a funny bun-"

Hinky Pinkies

What do you call a rabbit comedian?
a funny, a funny, a funny bunny

What do you call a goofy goat?
a silly, a silly, a silly billy

What do you call a beautiful cat?
a pretty, a pretty, a pretty kitty

What do you call a larger shovel?
a bigger, a bigger, a bigger digger!

What do you call an improved note?
a better, a better, a better letter!

What do you call a hummingbird in July?
a summer, a summer, a summer hummer.

Funny Bunny

Here's a silly fellow with consonant sounds in the middle of his name. Hold up your sample and say that this is everybody's favorite long-eared comedian, Funny Bunny. Ask students which consonant they hear in the middle of both funny and bunny. Emphasize the sound so it is hard to miss. They should say N.

Figure 2.41 A Photograph of Funny Bunny

Materials:
- copies of Funny Bunny Pattern
- sample bunny
- scissors
- crayons or markers
- tape, staples, or glue

Procedure:
- Cut out the bunny, including the long tabs, along the lines. Cut the feet apart on the center line.
- Paste, tape, or staple the ends of the tabs together to form a cylindrical stand.
- Fold the feet forward.

From the Studio:
Other middle consonant art activities include puppets, quilling (coiled spring-like strips of paper glued down to create a design), pulled string paintings (Dip string in tempera and pull it across the page.) and spatter painting (with tempera, a toothbrush and a piece of window screen). Keeping the rabbit theme, use the headband concept (see Goggles) to make bunny ears or design a paper plate bunny mask.

Funny Bunny Pattern

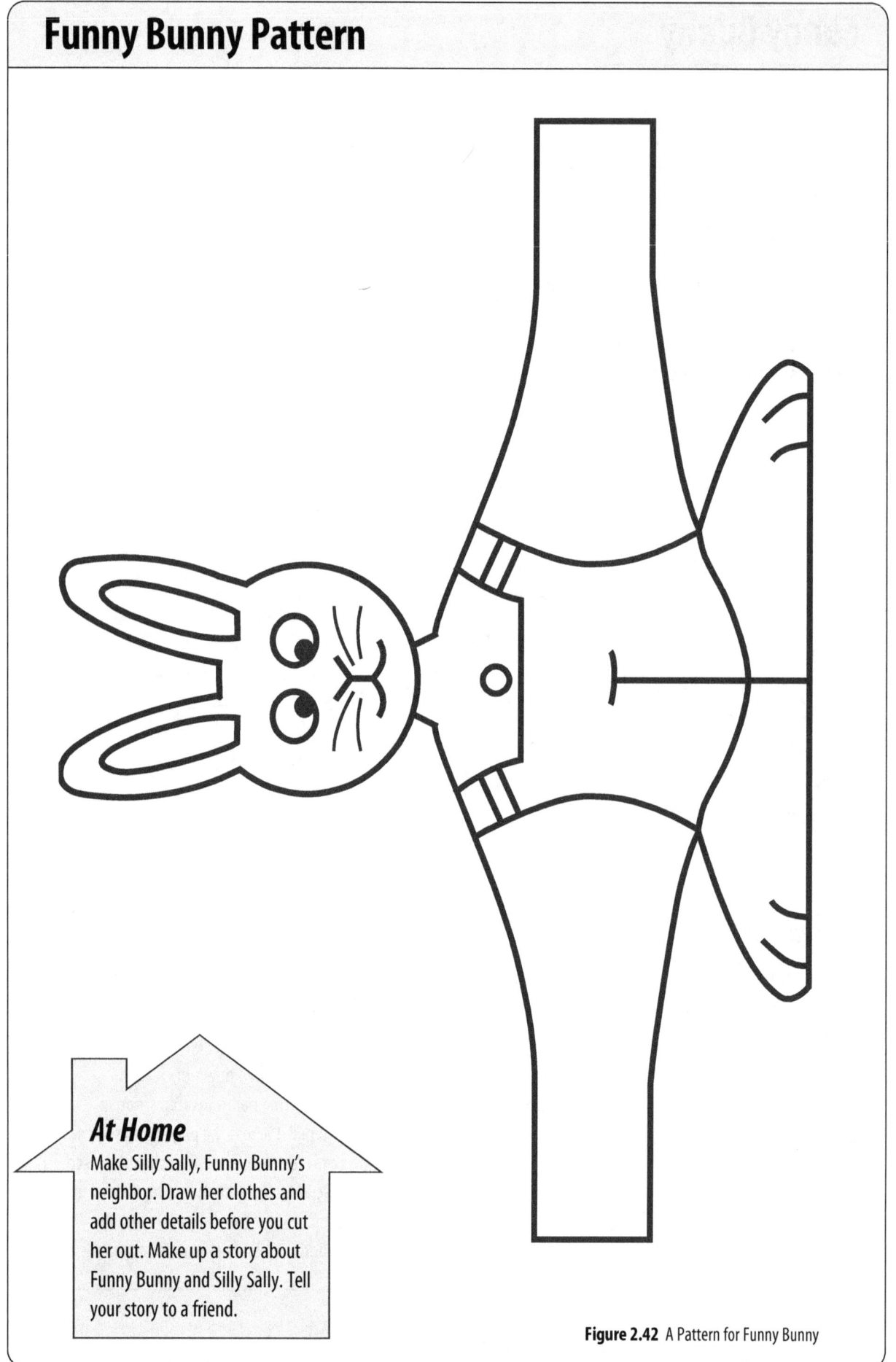

At Home
Make Silly Sally, Funny Bunny's neighbor. Draw her clothes and add other details before you cut her out. Make up a story about Funny Bunny and Silly Sally. Tell your story to a friend.

Figure 2.42 A Pattern for Funny Bunny

SECTION 3
Vowels

INTRODUCTION

Long and short vowels make words sing. Without vowels, we could not say words.

Tr ths!

If the vowels were there, it would say Try this! You might have guessed the content of the little sentence, but you could not say it aloud without adding vowel sounds.

Vowels are the sounds that singers hold on long notes. Like all things that are often used, vowels are complex and quirky. Each vowel letter represents many different sounds, but some are more common than others.

The first vowel sounds children usually learn are the short sounds of a, e, i, o, and u. These sounds are found not only in consonant-vowel-consonant words, such as *run, set,* or *hot,* but also in the C-V-C pattern syllables of such complex words as *consonant* and *consider*.

Beginning readers also learn a second set of vowel sounds, the long vowels. Long vowel sounds are easier to remember than short vowel sounds because they match their letter names. For example, a long A sounds like a. Unfortunately, long vowel spellings can be confusing. For example, the long O sound can be spelled oa as in boat, ow as in snow, oe as in toe, ough as in though, or oh, as in Oh! The long vowel letter combination taught first is the C-V-C-E, or consonant-vowel-consonant-E, configuration. It appears in such kindergarten and first grade words as *came, home, time,* and *tune*.

Both C-V-C and C-V-C-E patterns are covered in *ABC, Follow Me!*

TEACHING IDEAS

Here are a few ideas for teaching or reviewing vowel sounds:

- Challenge participants to provide rhymes for words you present.
- Use word walls to introduce or review pattern words such as bit, fit, hit, lit, and pit.
- Pose riddles. The answers should be words with a featured vowel sound. For example, if I were teaching long O, I might say, "I am what you leave in the morning and go back to in the afternoon. I have rooms inside, and you live in me. I rhyme with roam. What am I?"

PICTURE BOOKS

Antle, Nancy, ill. John Sandford. *The Good Bad Cat*. Grand Haven, Mich.: School Zone Pub. Co., 1985.

Cameron, Alice, ill. Carol Jones. *The Cat Sat on the Mat.*; Boston: Houghton Mifflin, 1994.

Coxe, Molly. *Big Egg*. New York: Random House, 2003.

Galdone, Paul. *The Little Red Hen*. New York: Clarion Books, 1973.

Hoff, Syd. *Mrs. Brice's Mice*. New York: HarperCollins, 1993.

Peet, Bill. *Zella, Zack, and Zodiac*. Boston: Houghton Mifflin, 1986.

Seuss, Dr. *The Cat in the Hat*. New York. Random House, 1957.

Snow, Pegeen and Robert Hillerich, ill. Tom Dunnington. *A Pet for Pat*. Chicago: Childrens Press, 1984.

WEB SITES

<<*http://www.songsforteaching.com/kidzup/vowels.htm*>>, "Songs for Teaching about vowels: Long and Short." There are many songs on this site. Have fun!

<<*http://www.glc.k12.ga.us/passwd/trc/ttools/attach/parent/10ways/TenWaysVowels.doc*>>, "Ten Ways to Practice Long and Short Vowel Sounds." Find practical teaching ideas here.

<<*http://www.teach-nology.com/worksheets/language_arts/phonics/vowels/id/I*>>, "Vowels: The Long and the Short!: I." Here's a nice illustrated worksheet to print.

<<*http://www.canteach.ca/elementary/songspoems35.html*>>, "Vowels" on the "Can Teach" site. Like to sing? Find songs to teach short and long vowels here.

<<*http://www.storyit.com/magnets/wmagnets.htm*>>, "Word Magnets," an activity for teaching short and long vowels inspired by a favorite refrigerator door pastime.

Unit 1: Short Vowels

NAT, NET, NOT, NUT! HOORAY FOR SHORT VOWELS! (C-V-C)

Before the session begins, use a marker and regular copy paper to make letter signs. There should be one large letter on each sheet. You will need separate signs for N, T, H, A, E, I, O, and U. Call seven volunteers to the front. Give one an N sign and another a T sign. Tell these consonant holders to face the group. There should enough room for another student to stand between them. The consonant carriers will remain in place while students holding various vowels move into the gap. Give each of the remaining volunteers a vowel card. Call the appropriate vowel before you start a verse, and wait for that volunteer to take his place. Each yell leader should lift his sign high over his head when his letter is called. Watch carefully and offer help when necessary.

Hints:
To allow for adequate practice, the chants and poems in this book have many verses. You do not have to share every stanza. The cheer Nat, Net, Not, Nut! demonstrates that changing just one letter, the vowel, can turn a net into a nut! If time is short, two or three of the verses should make the point.

Nat, Net, Not, Nut!

Leader: Give me an N! (students repeat)

Leader: Give me an A! (students repeat)

Leader: Give me a T! (students repeat)

N-A-T! (Students repeat, as letter holders lift all three letters at the same time.)
Nat! (students repeat) Who's that? (students repeat)
(Follow the same pattern for each verse.)
Give me an N! Give me an E!
Give me a T!

N-E-T! Net! Fish in a net.
Give me an N! Give me an O!
Give me a T!

N-O-T! Not! Won't; will not.
Give me an N! Give me a U!
Give me a T!

N-U-T! Nut! Crack a nut.
(Trade the N for an H)
Give me an H! Give me an a!
Give me a T!

H-A-T! Hat! Put on a hat.
Give me an H! Give me an I!
Give me a T!

H-I-T! Hit! Hit that ball!
Give me an H! Give me an O!
Give me a T!

H-O-T! Hot! Summer is hot!
Give me an H! Give me a U!
Give me a T!

H-U-T! Hut! He lives in a hut.
Nat, net, not, nut; hat, hit, hot, hut,
Short vowels! Short vowels!
Hip, hip, hooray!

Word Bugs Project

Figure 3.1 A Photograph of the Finished Ladybug

Ladybugs are beautiful, gentle, and easy to find. In this project, they represent the short U sound in bug.

Materials:
- copies of A Lady Bug Pattern
- crayons or markers
- scissors
- sample ladybug

From the Studio:

Using Ed Emberley's drawing books as inspiration, encourage students to make fingerprint bugs.

Procedure:

- Write the word bug on the board. Invite students to sound it out one letter at a time, and then have them name some bugs.
- Show the sample ladybug.
- Distribute the materials.
- Encourage students to color the ladybug.
- Demonstrate how to cut it out.
- Fold the legs down, and then fold the feet out.

A Lady Bug Pattern

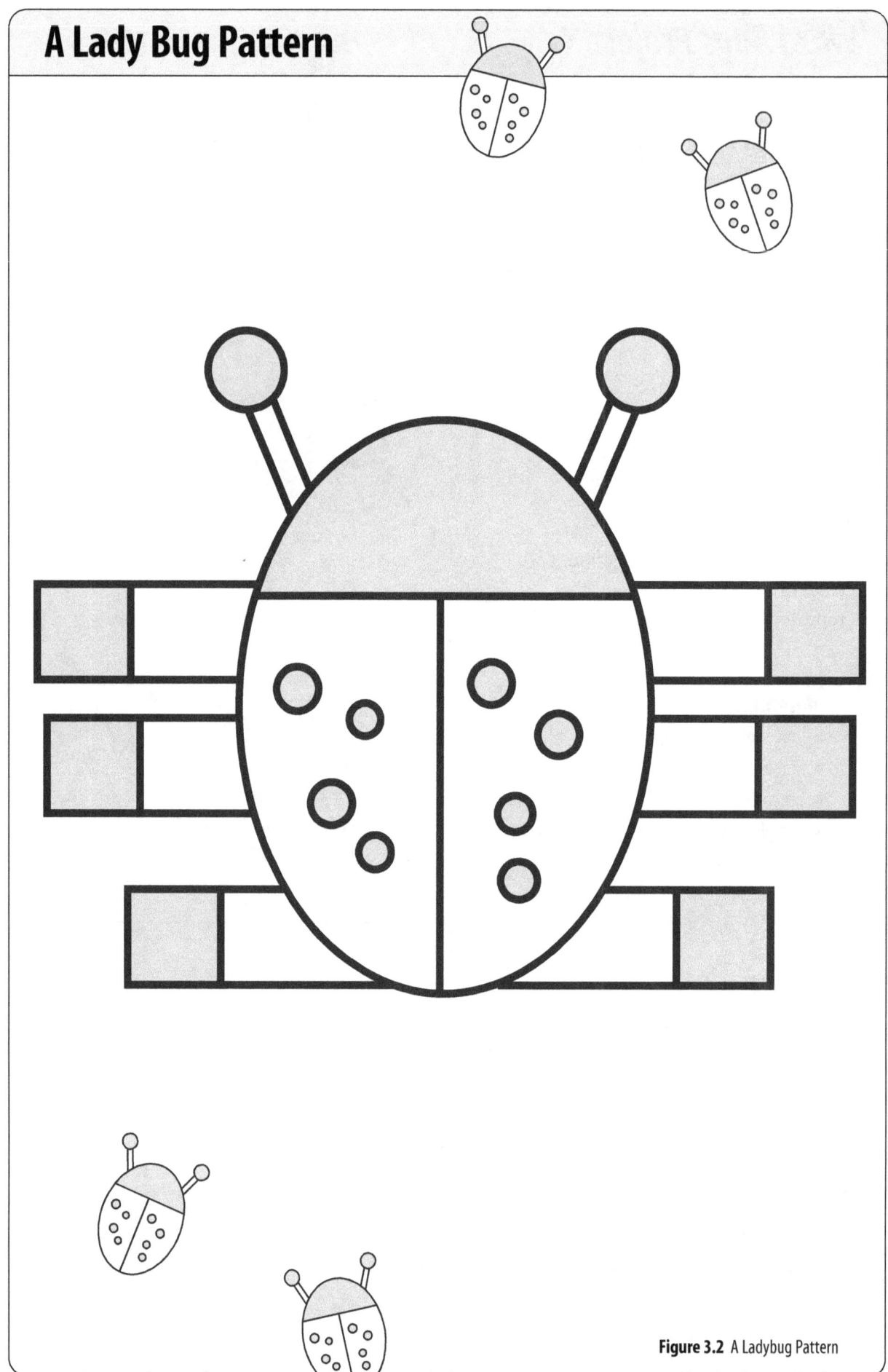

Figure 3.2 A Ladybug Pattern

Unit 2: Short A

A FLAT BAT AND OTHER SHORT A'S

Here's an introduction to the short A sound. Before presenting the rhyme, write the letter Aa on the board. Challenge participants to name the letter. Explain that it often stands for the sound heard at the beginning of the word apple. Encourage students to repeat the first line of each stanza after you.

Cat, Hat, Pan, Bat

That's a cat, not a cot.
It purrs and it naps.
It begs for pats
And it sits on laps.

That's a hat, not a hut.
You put it on your head.
You wear it in the sun,
But never in bed.

That's a pen, not a pan.
It writes with ink.
My Dad likes black,
And my sister likes pink.

That's a bat, not a bit.
It flies in the dark.
It lives in a cave
At the county park.

Section 3: Vowels

A Flat Bat Craft Project

Here's a deliciously creepy project that reviews the short A sound.

Figure 3.3 A Photograph of a Finished Bat

Materials:
- A copy of "Flat Bat Pattern"
- a sample flapping bat
- scissors
- crayons or markers

From the Studio:

Other possible short A projects include Colored Place Mats, Craft Clay Animals, and Accordion Folded Fans. For some great Wax Paper art ideas, see *Preschool Art: It's the Process not the Product* by Maryann Kohl. The projects are great for all primary grades.

Procedure:

- Review the short sound of the vowel A. Challenge students to remember some short A words from the poem.
- Show the sample bat.
- Demonstrate how to color and cut out the bat.
- Distribute materials.
- Walk around to punch holes for string.
- Fold the bat in the center to punch the holes.
- Loop string through the holes.

Flat Bat Pattern

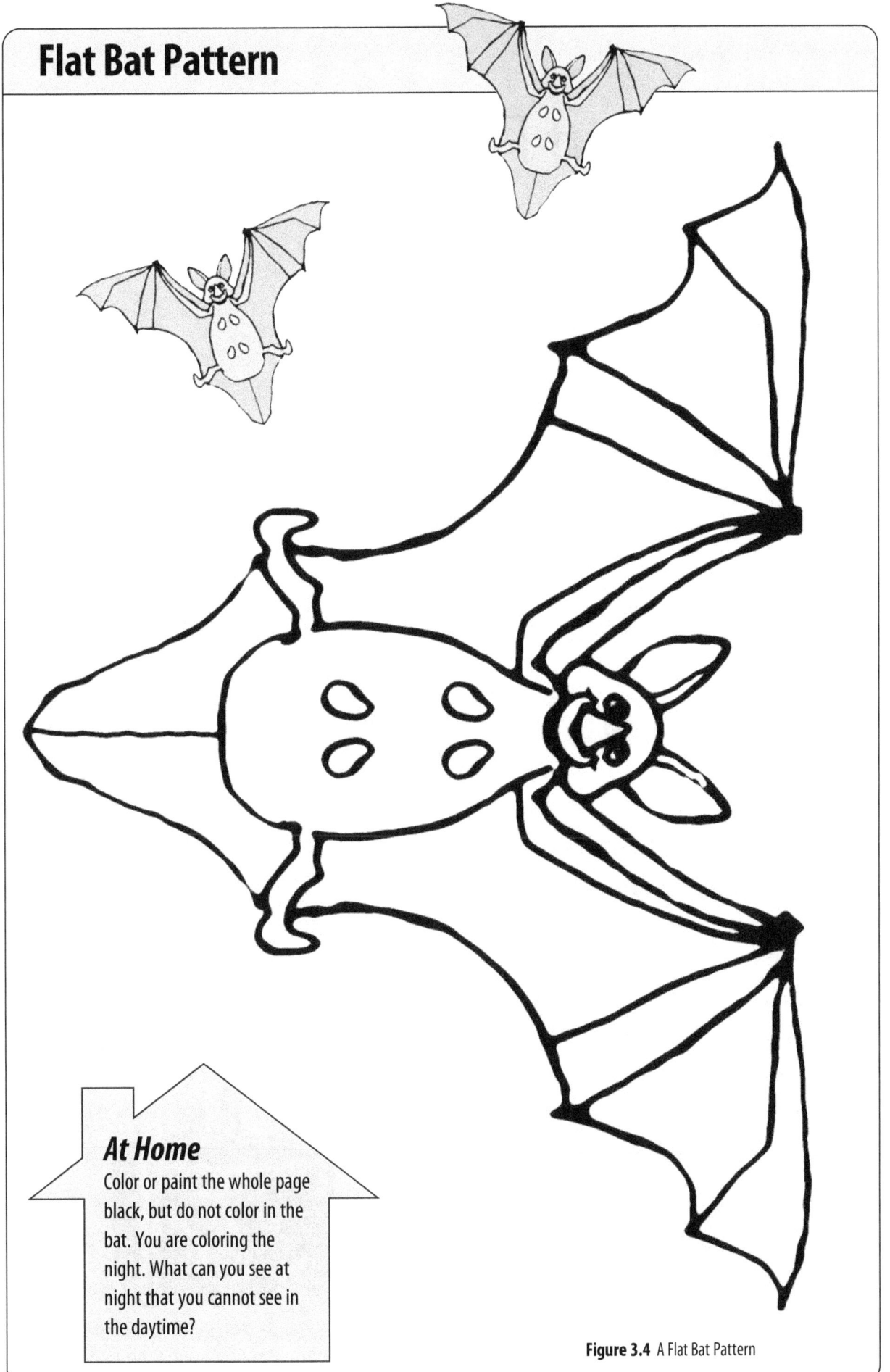

At Home
Color or paint the whole page black, but do not color in the bat. You are coloring the night. What can you see at night that you cannot see in the daytime?

Figure 3.4 A Flat Bat Pattern

Unit 3: Short E

Red Leg Web Neb: A Nonsense Verse

Here is a lively verse composed entirely of short E syllables. Write the letter Ee on the board. Ask students to name it. Then, tell them E often stands for the sound heard at the beginning of the word elephant.

Hints: Create similar nonsense rhymes for other short vowels.

Red, Leg, Web, Neb

Leader: Bet, let, met, wet
Participants: wet, wet, wet, wet
Leader: Ten, pen, den, men
Participants: men, men, men, men
Leader: Bed, fed, led, red
Participants: red, red, red, red
Leader: Beg, leg, egg, peg
Participants: peg, peg, peg, peg
Leader: Bell, fell, tell, well
Participants: well, well, well, well
Less, mess, guess, yes,
yes, yes, yes, yes!

Magic Red: A Red and Green Vibrating Target

Here's a classic color exercise that seems like real magic. When you stare at a brilliant hue, such as red, for a minute or so, and then close your eyes, you will see its complement. Try it!

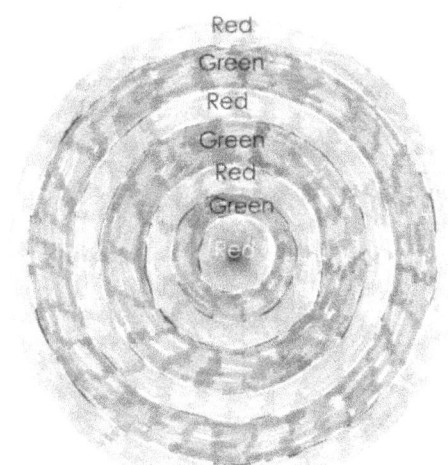

Figure 3.1 A Scan of a Finished Red and Green Target

Materials:
- copies of A Red and Green Target Pattern
- a sheet of bright green and a sheet of bright red construction paper
- markers or crayons in bright red and green (should be close to the same value)
- a finished sample of the Red and Green Target project

for the "From the Studio" project:
- red and green tempera, water, brushes, paper

> **From the Studio:**
> Use tempera and brushes to make complementary spatter paintings.

Procedure:
- Review the short E sound. Encourage students to recall some short E words from the verse.
- Explain that sometimes your eyes can be fooled. These tricks are called "optical illusions."
- Optional: Share a book with large illustrations of common optical illusions.
- Say that one kind of optical illusion depends on colors. If certain colors, called "complementary colors" are placed beside each other, they can cause a vibration or dancing white light where they meet.
- Call two volunteers to the front of the room. Give one volunteer the red. Invite participants to name the color.
- Tell students to stare at the red paper without blinking. Time it. They should stare for a full thirty seconds. When they close their eyes, they should see a green square.
- Give your other volunteer the sheet of green paper. Encourage the two students to put their papers beside each other so the group can see the effect.
- Share the sample target.
- Distribute materials.
- Encourage students to color the target. Alternating circles should be red and green.
- When participants finish, encourage them to stare at the target. After 30 seconds, they should be able to see the target with the colors reversed. Invite them to share the effect with friends and family.

Magic Red Pattern

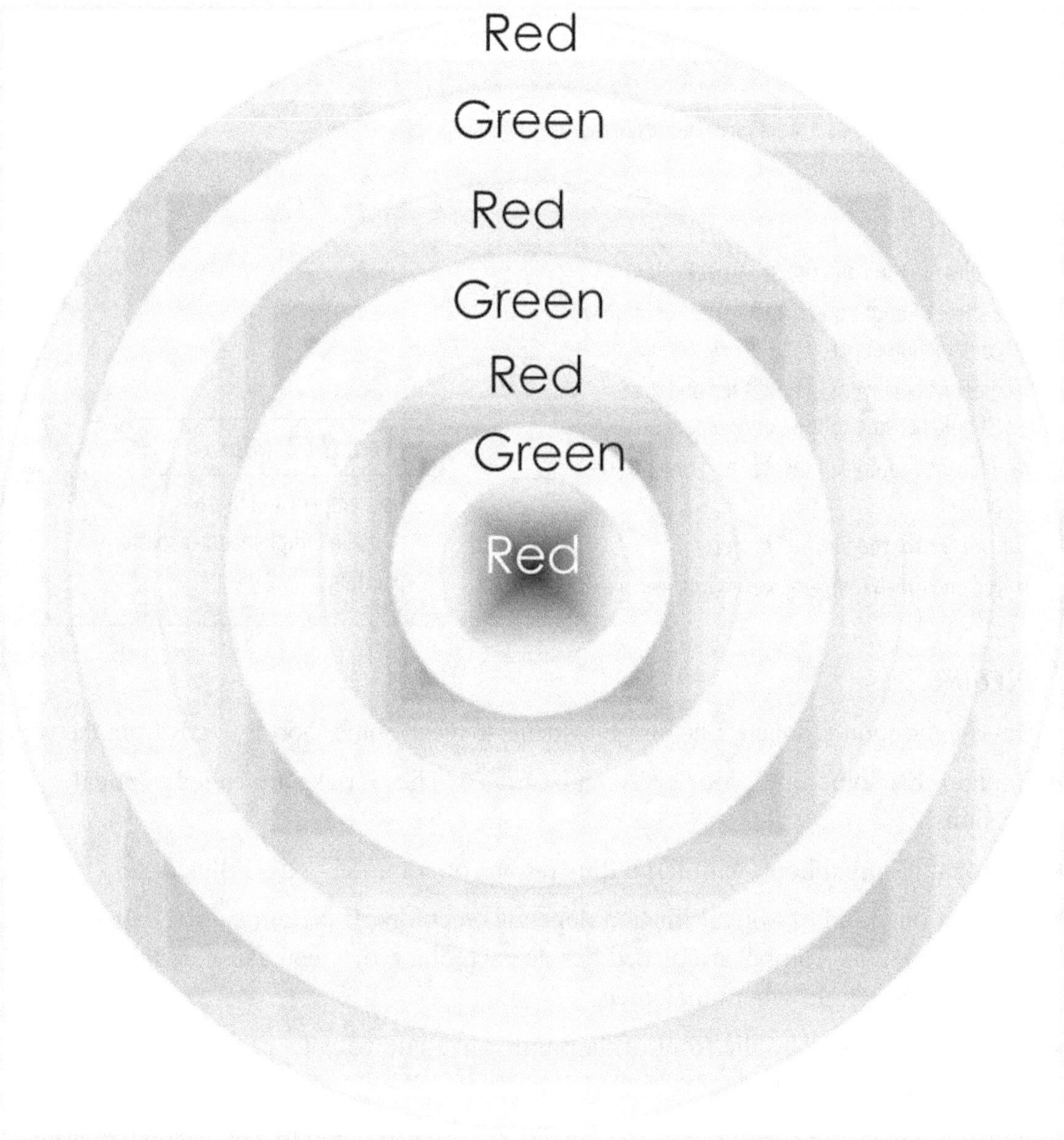

Red

Green

Red

Green

Red

Green

Red

At Home
Well is a short E word. Pretend the target is the inside of a wishing well. Color the outside ring light blue. Color each ring inside a darker blue. After you color the middle, make a wish. Wish is a short I word!

Figure 3.6 A Red and Green Target Pattern

ABC, Follow Me! Phonics Rhymes and Crafts, Grades K-1

Unit 4: Short I

Inkso, Blinkso, I Don't Think So!

Write the letter I on the board. Explain that it often stands for the sound heard at the beginning of the word insect. Tell students that you are going to say three words. One of them has the I sound. Challenge them to raise their hands when they hear it. Tell them to listen the first time and raise their hands for the correct word the second time.

Say: hat hit hot. Pause after each word. Repeat. Next, introduce Inkso, Blinkso, I don't think so! Rehearse the repeating line several times before presenting the poem.

Encourage students to join in at the end of each stanza.

In, in, insect. Is a fish an insect?
Participants: Inkso, blinkso, I don't think so!

Ill, ill, bill. Does a pig have a bill?
Participants: Inkso, blinkso, I don't think so!

Ib, ib, rib. Does a worm have a rib?
Participants: Inkso, blinkso, I don't think so!

Ig, ig, wig. Does a horse wear a wig?
Participants: Inkso, blinkso, I don't think so!

In, in, chin. Does a mushroom have a chin?
Participants: Inkso, blinkso, I don't think so!

Ip, ip, lip. Does a bird have a lip?
Participants: Inkso, blinkso, I don't think so!

Id, id, kid. Is a baby cow a kid?
Participants: Inkso, blinkso, I don't think so!

Ick, ick, tick. Does a dog say "tick?"
Participants: Inkso, blinkso, I don't think so!

Ish, ish, wish. Can you make a wish?
Participants: Inkso, blinkso, yes, I think so.

Something Fishy: A Mobile

Two fish swim through an air ocean as part of this short I coat hanger mobile.

Figure 3.7 A Photograph of a Finished Fish Mobile

Materials:
- copies of Something Fishy: A Mobile Pattern
- markers or crayons
- scissors
- light string or heavy thread (crochet weight)
- a coat hanger (any kind) for each mobile

For "From the Studio":
- Colored tissue paper, liquid starch, individual containers, brushes, white paper

From the Studio:
Cut or tear fish shapes out of different shades of colored tissue paper. The fish do not have to be perfect. Lay them down on a sheet of white paper. Parts of different fish should overlap. Paint over them with starch. Where tissue fins overlap, colors will mix.

Procedure:

- Review the short I sound. Print Ii on the board. Encourage students to recall some short I words from the verse.
- Ask students what swims in the sea, starts with an F, and is a short I word.
- Show them the sample mobile.
- Distribute the materials.
- Show them how to color, and then cut out the fish.
- Walk around to punch holes in the fish and add the string. In the library, enlist the help of parents. In the classroom, collect the fish and assemble the mobiles later.

Fish Patterns for the Mobile or for Coloring

At Home
Make a barbequed fish dish. Color one of the fish brown. Add grill marks. Glue it to a paper plate. Add pictures of your favorite potatoes and vegetables to the plate.

Figure 3.8 Fish patterns for the mobile or for coloring

Unit 5: Short O

THE BLOB: SHORT O

To introduce the lesson, write the letter Oo on the board and encourage participants to name it. Explain that o can represent the sound heard at the beginning of the word *octopus*. Tell students that you are going to say a word. If it has the sound of o heard at the beginning of the word octopus, they should form an o with the thumb and forefinger of their right hand. If it does not have the sound of o, they should keep their hands folded. Then, say the following words, one at a time, giving group members time to respond: hot, dog, cat, mop, job, top, ten, hop, pan, not, pop.

Next, introduce the verse. Practice the clapping pattern before adding the words. Simplify as needed, for example, you might choose to clap all the way through, skipping the slaps and snaps.

Leader: Short o: nod

Participants: Short o: nod

Leader: Hod, mod, mod

Participants: Hod, mod, mod

Leader: Short o: Stop!

(Put up both hands facing the audience when you say "Stop!"

The Blob

Mark each beat with a slap, clap, or snap. Say one word per beat.

Leader: Short o: Tom. (Slap, clap, snap, or Slap, clap, clap)

Participants: Short o: Tom (Slap, clap, snap, or Slap, clap, clap)

Leader: Hom, mom, mom. (Slap, clap, snap, or Slap, clap, clap)

Participants: Hom, mom, mom. (Slap, clap, snap, or Slap, clap, clap)

(Continue the clapping pattern.)

Leader: Short o: fox

Participants: Short o: fox

Leader: hox, mox, mox

Participants: hox, mox, mox

Leader: Short o: Tom

Participants: Short o: Tom

Leader: Hom, mom, mom

Participants: Hom, mom, mom

Leader: Short o: dot

Participants: Short o: dot

Leader: Hot, mot, mot

Participants: Hot, mot, mot

Leader: Short o: nod

Participants: Short o: nod

Leader: Hod, mod, mod

Participants: Hod, mod, mod

Leader: Short o: Stop!

(Put up both hands facing the audience when you say "Stop!"

The Blob: An Art Project

Figure 3.9 A Scan of a Finished Blob Drawing

Materials:
- copies of Pattern for a Blob
- crayons or markers

From the Studio:

Anytime you have a few minutes and want to do an art activity, encourage students to make a scribble. (It must be a closed shape like the blob.) Then, instruct participants to add details to make the shape into something. Collect the drawings and staple them together into a book. Use the book to inspire discussions in small groups.

Procedure:

- Review the short O sound. Encourage participants to name words containing the short O sound.
- Show students the blob. Tell them it is a picture of something. Ask them what it is. Take suggestions. Then, explain that there are no correct or incorrect solutions.
- Distribute materials.
- Encourage students to decide what their blob is and then finish the picture.
- Invite volunteers to show their pictures and talk about them.

The Blob Pattern

At Home
Tell someone a story about your blob drawing. What is happening in the picture?

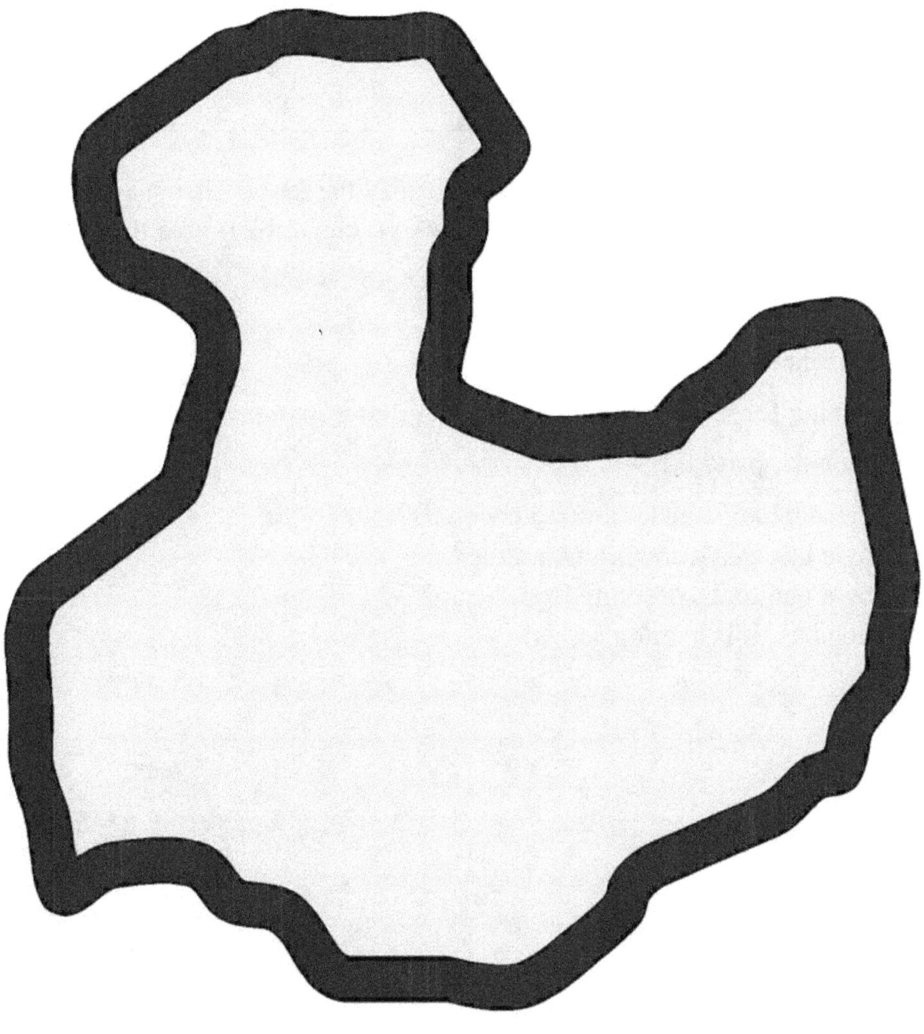

Figure 3.10 A Blob Pattern

Unit 6: Short U

Where is the Bus?

Write Uu on the board. Invite participants to identify the letter. Then, say that u can stand for the sound at the beginning of the word up. As you read the rhyme that follows, encourage students to echo each short U word.

Leader: Where is the bus. *Participants:* bus

Leader: Is it coming for us? *Participants:* us

(Please continue the pattern.)

Is it rolling by some huts made of dried coconuts?
Is it rolling by a bug that's crawling on a rug?
Is it rolling by a pup that's drinking from a cup?
Here comes the bus. It is coming for us!

Cut It Out!

The word cut is built around a short U. Here's a paper cutting project. The cutting lines on the pattern are only suggestions. Instruct participants to cut out a few holes, or many, depending on the patience and coordination of your group. Remember, cutting practice and symmetry discoveries are more important than perfect results.

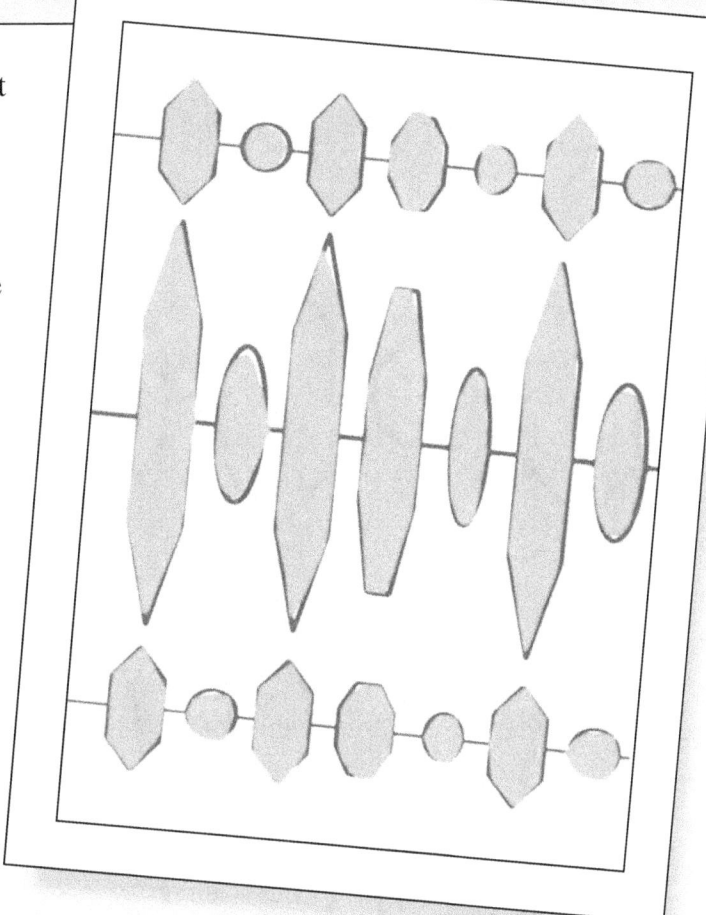

Figure 3.11 A Scan of Finished Paper Lace

Materials:
- copies of A Paper Lace Pattern
- scissors

Procedure:
- Review the short U sound. Encourage students to recall some of the short U sounds from the poem.
- Show the group the finished sample.
- Demonstrate how to fold and cut the paper.
- Pass out the pattern page. Help students fold it. They should fold the paper in half with the cutting lines on the outside.
- Cut along the lines. You will be cutting out pieces along the fold.
- Unfold to see the results.

From the Studio:

If the group is advanced, show them how to cut along the other two lines. Other possible short U art projects include stick puppets, rubbings, and rubber stamping.

Paper Lace Pattern

Figure 3.12 A Paper Lace Pattern

At Home
Color the shapes in the paper lace pattern to make a design. Use only two or three colors. Fold a sheet of paper. Cut your own paper lace design. Remember to cut your shapes out of the folded edge.

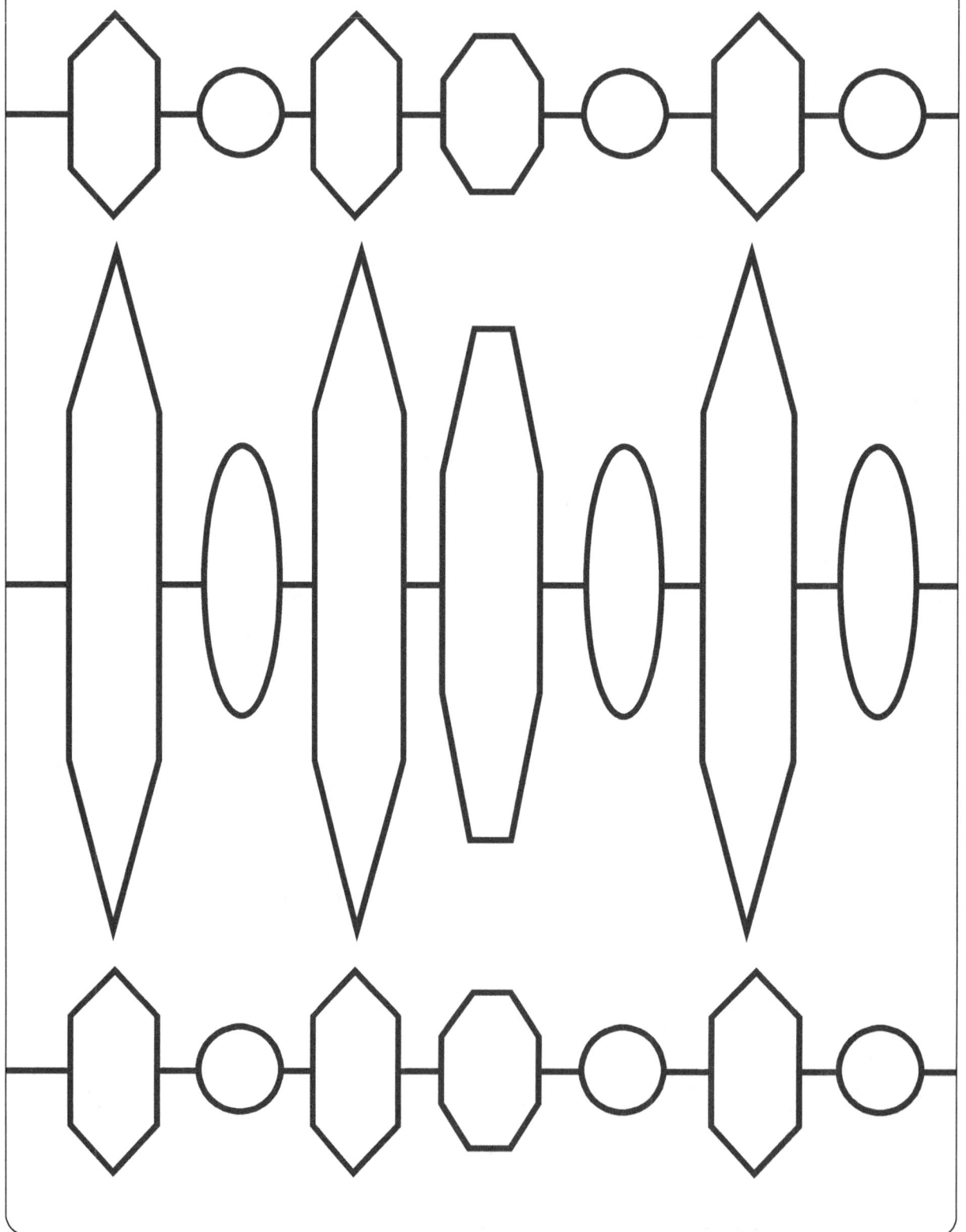

Unit 7: Long Vowels

THE VOWEL SAYS ITS NAME

This verse introduces or reviews five long vowel sounds. Write the letters a, e, i, o, and u on the board. Explain that they are vowels, and they can represent more than one sound. Remind participants that they have studied the short vowel sounds.

Explain that, today, they will start studying long vowel sounds. Encourage them to name each letter, and then congratulate them on being so smart. Tell them that they have already learned the long vowel sounds! Then, present the verse. Visual association is crucial for the mastery of this skill. Write each word on a chart or the board as you say it, or use pre-made word cards.

The Short and Long of It

Leader: Short a in can, but long A in cane
When E's at the end, the vowel says its name.
Short E in the, but long E in these
When an E's at the end, say a long vowel, please.
Short I in Tim, but long I in time.
When an E's at the end, dim becomes dime.
Short o in not, but long in note.
When an E's at the end, o gets the vote.
Short u in cut, but long U in cute.
When an E's at the end, that final E's mute.
Five different vowels: One rule that's the same.
When an E's at the end, the vowel says its name.
(Repeat the verse, encouraging students to read the words you write or display.)

A Note Card: A Long Vowel Art Project

Long O is right at home in the word *note*! Modify this simple note card design to fit any season.

Figure 3.13 A Scan of a Finished Note Card

Materials:
- copies of A Note Card Pattern
- a finished note card
- markers or crayons
- scissors
- clear tape or large self-adhesive dots

Procedure:

- Review the long vowel sounds. Encourage students to name long vowel words from the verse.
- Show the sample note card.
- Demonstrate how to color, cut out, and fold the card.
- Distribute materials and help students make the cards.
- Help students print I like you! or a seasonal message inside the card.
- If students print or draw inside the card, make each note private. Seal the greeting with a little piece of clear tape or a self-adhesive dot.

From the Studio:

Make a card for a special holiday, such as a picture book writer's birthday.

A Note Card Pattern

At Home
Use the pattern to make four or five blank note cards for your mother or your aunt. Draw a different picture on the front of each card. Stack the finished cards up and wrap a ribbon around them. Fasten the ends of the ribbon with a little piece of tape. Add a small sticky bow.

Figure 3.14 Note Card Pattern

Unit 8: Long A

Long A, as in Snake: A Cumulative Rhyme

This little verse plays with the long A sound. To introduce it, write Aa on the board and encourage the group to name the letter. Remind students that a can represent the sound they hear at the beginning of the word ace. Next, teach them the repeating line, dake, hake, nake-ee—oh; a string of nonsense words with the C-V-C-E pattern. As the cumulative rhyme continues, encourage participants to anticipate each upcoming line.

Dake, Hake, Nake-ee-Oh!

Leader: There's a S-S-snake beside the lake.

Participants: dake, hake, nake-ee—oh

Leader: There's a S-S-snake near the lane beside the lake.

Participants: dake, hake, nake-ee—oh

Leader: There's a S-S-snake under the gate near the lane beside the lake.

Participants: dake, hake, nake-ee—oh

Leader: There's a snake among the grapes under the gate near the lane beside the lake

Participants: dake, hake, nake-ee—oh

Leader: There's a snake in the glade among the grapes under the gate near the lane beside the lake

Participants: dake, hake, nake-ee—oh

ABC, Follow Me! Phonics Rhymes and Crafts, Grades K-1

Snakes!

Here's a springy cut-and-color project that requires no glue and produces no scraps! It's a great accompaniment to Tomi Ungerer's classic *Crictor*, or *Snakes* by Seymour Simon.

Figure 3.15 A Photograph of a Finished Spiral Snake

Materials:

- sample spiral snake
- copies of A Paper Snake Pattern
- markers or crayons
- scissors

Procedure:

- Review the sound of long A. Encourage students to name long A words or nonsense syllables from the verse.
- Show participants the sample snake.
- Show them how to color the snake.
- Demonstrate how to cut the spiral.
- Pull up the springy snake! Hiss menacingly.
- Distribute materials.
- Walk around and help students start their cuts, if necessary.

From the Studio:

Craft clay snakes are easy to make. They are also good practice for later coil clay pots. Use your favorite craft clay recipe, or use a commercial product. Give the children balls of clay and encourage them to make snakes!

Hints:

Here's a simple craft clay recipe:

- 1 part flour
- 1 part salt
- Add water a little at a time and knead to a clay consistency.
- Store in a sealed plastic bag in the refrigerator.

Find more clay recipes at

\>>*http://www.kidsturncentral.com/crafts/crecipe19.htm*>>
\>>*http://www.archjrc.com/childsplace/craft.html*>>
\>>*http://www.canadianparents.com/CPO/CanadaCooks/ CraftRecipes/2004/05/12/456758.html*>>

or search for "children's craft clay recipes."

Paper Snake Pattern Page

At Home
Give your paper snake a name. Make a house for him out of a shoebox. Glue pictures to the outside and the inside of the box. Make up some stories about your snake.

Figure 3.16 A Paper Snake Pattern

Unit 9: Long I

Let's Take a Hike!

This is a long I version of a summer camp favorite, "The Lion Hunt." In this North American verse, the lion has become a bear, and he is not being hunted. Hikers meet him when they pass his home, an old mine. The basic movement is "walking," or slapping one knee and then the other. "Walk" slowly on the way up the hill, and quickly on the way down. There is an introduction, which includes many long I words. In this first section, participants "drive" to the trailhead at a place called White Pines. If time or attention are in short supply, skip to the beginning of the hike.

Introduction

Leader: Let's take a hike.

Participants: Let's take a hike.

Leader: Drive to White Pines.

Participants: Drive to White Pines.

Leader: Drive for nine miles.

Participants: Drive for nine miles.

Leader: What a long ride!

Participants: What a long ride!

Leader: Here we are.

Participants: Here we are.

Leader: Lock the car.

Participants: Lock the car.

Let's Take a Hike: *(Start here for the short version.)*

Leader: The trail isn't wide.
Participants: The trail isn't wide.
Leader: Let's form a line.
Participants: Let's form a line.
Leader: Hike past that pine.
Participants: Hike past that pine.
Leader: Push back the vine.
Participants: Push back the vine.
Leader: Shh! A bee hive.
Participants: Shh! A bee hive.
Leader: There's an old mine.
Participants: There's an old mine.
Leader: What is inside?
Participants: What is inside?
Leader: What's tall and wide?
Participants: What's tall and wide?
Leader: What has a lot of hair?
Participants: What has a lot of hair?
Leader: Don't be afraid. It's only a B—
Participants: A bear!
Leader: Uh oh! Time to go!
Participants: Uh oh! Time to go!
Leader: Tiptoe past the bees. (Repeat each previous motion, faster.)
Participants: Tiptoe past the bees.
Leader: Push back the vine.
Participants: Push back the vine.
Leader: Run past the pine.
Participants: Run past the pine.
Leader: I see the car.
Participants: I see the car.
Leader: It isn't far.
Participants: It isn't far.
Leader: Whew!
Participants: Whew!
Leader: We went on a hike.
Participants: We went on a hike.
Leader: We had a good time.
Participants: We had a good time.
Leader: That's the end of the rhyme.

Kite Bookmarks

Spring is a great time for hikes. It is also a great time for flying kites. Make these pretty bookmarks to celebrate the season while reviewing the long I sound.

Materials:
- a finished kite bookmark
- copies of "The Kite Pattern"
- scissors
- markers
- glue sticks

Procedure:

- Review the long I sound. Encourage students to recall some long I words from "Let's Take a Hike."
- Show the sample kite bookmark.
- Demonstrate how to color the kite and the bows.
- Cut out all of the parts. Paste the end of the tail to the back of the base of the kite.
- Paste the other kite to the back, making the pasted end of the tail into the center of a sandwich.
- Paste the bows at intervals along the tail.
- You may use ribbon strips instead of the paper tails, if desired.

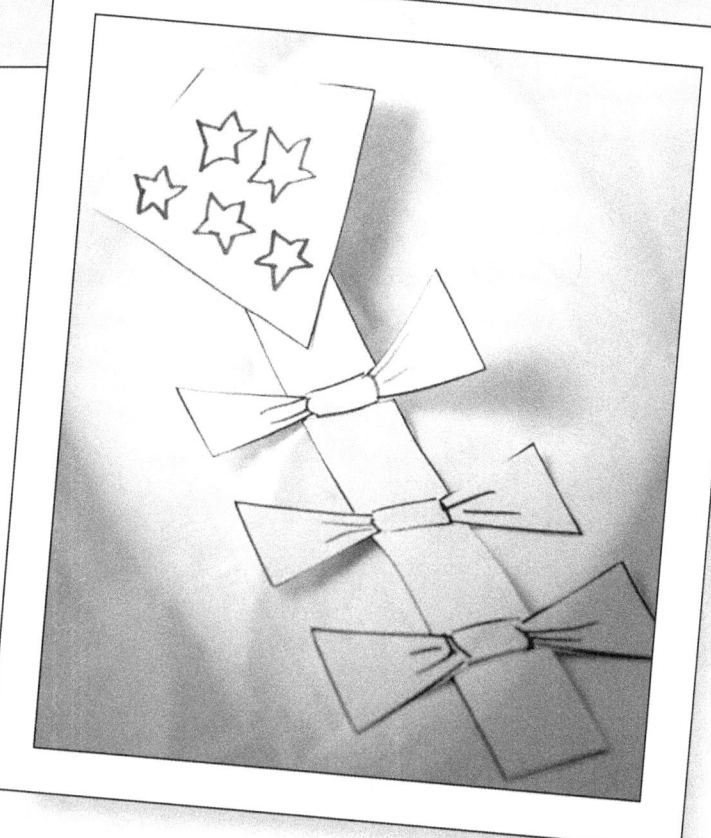

Figure 3.17 A Scan of a Finished Kite Bookmark

From the Studio:

Make a kite that really flies. Here are some sites with classroom tested designs!

- <<*http://www.aloha.net/%7Ebigwind/20kidskites.html*>>
  Big Wind Kite Factory, Molokai, Hawaii presents: 20 Kids * 20 Kites * 20 Minutes
- <<*http://www.kites.org/zoo/class.html*>>
  The Virtual Kite Zoo: Kites in the Classroom. Here's a fine collection of kite making links.
- <<*http://stepbystepcc.com/kites2.html*>>
  Kite Theme: Look here to find instructions and links for kite-related classroom projects.
- <<*http://www.ed.uri.edu/unitweb/dennis/sledkitepattern.htm*>>
  Here you will find a springtime bulletin board plan and a great collection of kite-making links. Choose the flying kite that works for your group.
- <<*http://www.ed.uri.edu/unitweb/dennis/sledkitepattern.htm*>>
  Find out how to make a simple sled kite.
- <<*http://www.ipl.org/div/kidspace/browse/fun1300/*>>
  This site has links to kite sites and to other paper craft sites, too!

A Kite Pattern

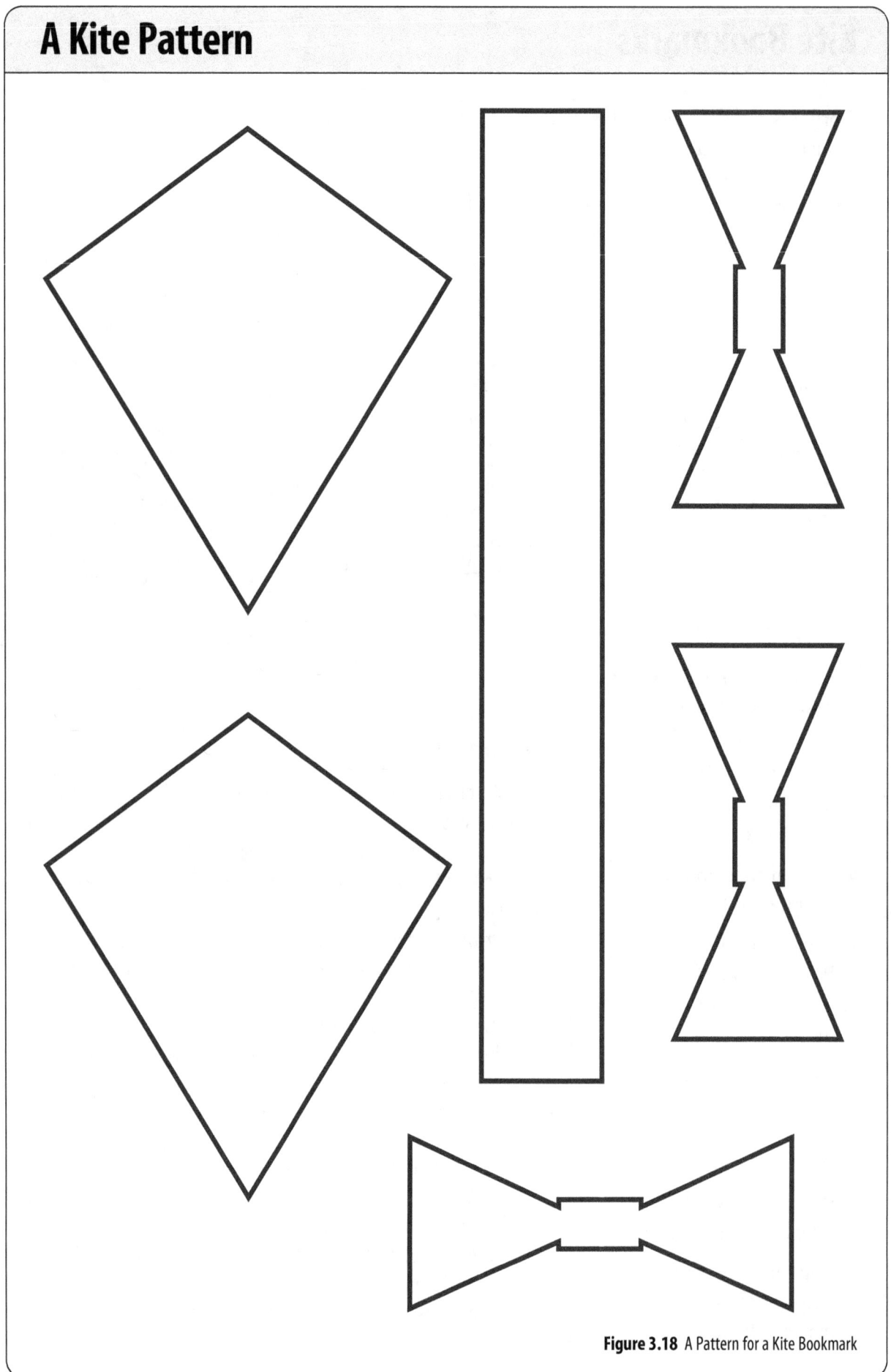

Figure 3.18 A Pattern for a Kite Bookmark

Unit 10: Long O

HOMES: A LONG O VERSE

Here's a verse to teach or review the long O sound. Combine it with books about houses and homes. Try *Wonderful Houses Around The World* by Yoshio Komatsu, ill. by Akira Nishiyama, trans. by Katy Bridges and Naoko Amemiya or *The Napping House* by Audrey Wood, ill. by Don Wood. When you present the verse, encourage students to listen for the word home in the poem and repeat it after you.

This Home, That Home

Leader: This home
Participants: home
Leader: has two stories. That home
Participants: home
Leader: has just one. This home
Participants: home
Leader: has a big backyard. That home
Participants: home
Leader: has none.
(Repeat the same pattern.)
This home has a tower.
That home has some swings.
This home has a fish pond
and other fancy things.
I do not need a boat house.
I do not need a dome.
Because the place my family lives
will always be my home.

A Drawing of Home

Develop memory and observation skills with this simple drawing task.

Figure 3.19 A Scan of a Sample House Drawing

Materials:
- markers or crayons
- paper
- (in the classroom) tempera, brushes, paper towels, and water

Procedure:
- Review the long O sound. Elicit long O words with riddles.
- Show a sample house drawing. Include details such as a porch, walkway, garage, driveway, windows, and door. It does not have to be a masterpiece.
- Distribute materials.
- Invite participants share their finished pictures and to tell what they like best about their homes.

From the Studio:
Use junk mail and catalogs to create a dream house collage. Tell students to draw a location such as the mountains or the beach. Use markers. Cut out a house, or parts of different houses, and paste the components to the background.

Long O Riddles:
- What starts with a B and is part of your skeleton?
- What starts with a Z and means part of a playing field?
- What starts with a V and means something your parents do on election day?
- What starts with an N and means a short written message?
- What starts with an H and means an empty space?

ABC, Follow Me! Phonics Rhymes and Crafts, Grades K-1

Unit 11: Long U

What's Missing? A Rhyme

Teach or review the long U sound. Invite students to finish each line of this rhyme. You may have to read the verse through twice before all participants chime in. If your listeners are first graders, consider making word cards for tune, June, cute, flute, mule, rule, cube, tube, pure, and sure.

Long U Music's a Tune

Long U music's a T-T-tune.

A long U month is J-J-June.

A puppy is long U C-C-cute,

and my sister plays a long U fl-fl-flute.

A prospector rides a long U M-M-mule.

Walking in halls is a long U R-R-rule.

A cardboard box is a long U C-C-cube

And a telescope's a long U T-T-tube.

Mountain water's long U P-P-pure

And I like you for long U S-S-sure!

Long U is in Blue

Figure 3.20 A Scan of a Sample Torn Paper Cloud Picture

Blue is a cool color. It also has a long U sound. To introduce this summery cut-and-paste project, tell participants to close their eyes. Invite them to imagine that it is a fine June or July day. They are lying on a grassy hill watching white clouds drift across the sky. When they open their eyes, share the classic picture book *It Looked Like Spilt Milk* by Charles G. Shaw. Read "Clouds" by Christina Rossetti. If desired, find other appropriate weather poems at >>*http://www.dcrafts.com/weatherpoems.htm*>>.

Materials:
- a sample torn paper cloud picture
- blue construction paper
- white paper
- scissors (optional)
- glue sticks

Procedure:

- Review the long U sound and encourage participants to recall long U words from the verse. Hold up a sheet of blue paper. Challenge students to name the color.
- Show the sample.
- Demonstrate how to tear cloud shapes from white paper. Tear slowly. Make rounded shapes.
- Glue the clouds to the paper.
- Distribute materials.
- Walk around and help students as needed.

From the Studio:
Give students an opportunity to paint clouds with tempera. When mixing paint, always add the darker color to the lighter color a little at a time until the desired color appears.

Appendix
Word Lists for Exercises, Verses, and Practice Cards

INITIAL CONSONANT WORDS

B: *Nouns:* boy, bat, ball, baby, bee, box, bird, bill, bus *Verbs:* begin, bat

C: *Nouns:* car, card, color, camp, country, can *Verbs:* call, come, carry, cut, collect

D: *Nouns:* day, door, deer, dragon *Verbs:* do, drink, draw, drop, dip

F: *Nouns:* foot, fork, fan, fish, fire, flower, face, family, food *Verbs:* fall, friend

G: *Nouns:* gas, glass, goat, girl, green, gate, gift *Verbs:* go, grow, give

H: *Nouns:* hand, hat, horse, house, home, ham, heart, horn *Verbs:* have, hit, honk

J: *Nouns:* jar, jet, jacks, jam, jewelry, jeans *Verbs:* jump, joke

K: *Nouns:* key, king, kite, kangaroo, kitten *Verbs:* kiss, kick

L: *Nouns:* leaf, ladder, lamp, lock, lamp, lion, lace, lake, lemon, lily *Verbs:* lean, like, learn, leave, lie, listen, lift

M: *Nouns:* milk, mouse, monkey, meat, mile, moose, mask, moon, money, mother *Verbs:* make, meet, miss, move

N: *Nouns:* name, nap, nine, number, nut, nest, nose *Verbs:* need

P: *Nouns:* pond, pool, pea, pod, peg, paw, peach, pen, pencil, penguin, penny, pet, pine *Verbs:* push, pin, pull

Q: *Nouns:* quail, quarter, question *Verbs:* quit

R: *Nouns:* rake, rag, rain, rice, race, ray, rug, rose *Verbs:* ride, roll, rise, ring, rub, race, run

S: *Nouns:* seed, sack, sand, sale, salt, seat, ship, shop, sign, shirt, shovel, snail, snake *Verbs:* save, stand, sit, soar, save, spin, sing

T: *Nouns:* tape, tail, tale, tea, tack, teacher, teeth, tent, tide, time, tools *Verbs:* tip, take, trade, trip, turn, twist, type

V: *Nouns:* vine, voice *Verbs:* view, visit

W: *Nouns:* weed, walnut, walrus, window, wood, woman *Verbs:* wake, wash, wear, wipe, watch, want, wait, wish, work, went

Y: *Nouns:* yard, year, yam, yucca *Verbs:* yell

Z: *Nouns:* zero, zipper, zebra, zoo *Verbs:* zip, zoom

Final X: fox, box, tax, wax, mix, fix, six

MEDIAL CONSONANT EXAMPLES:

hobby, daddy, mommy, muddy, bunny, funny, sunny, happy, puppy, poppy, kitty

SHORT VOWELS IN CONSONANT-VOWEL-CONSONANT WORDS

A: bat, cat, fat, hat, mat, pat, rat, sat, vat, cab, lab, tab, bad, had, sad, mad, bag, rag, tag, dam, ham, jam, can, fan, ran, ban, cap, lap, map, nap, tap

E: beg, keg, bed, fed, red, wed, bet, let, met, net, pet, set, wet, ten, men, pen

I: bib, rib, bid, did, hid, kid, lid, big, dig, fig, pig, wig, fin, bin, pin, tin, win, dip, hip, lip, tip, sip, bit, kit, fit, hit, lit, pit, sit

O: son, got, dot, hot, not, pot, tot, box, fox, job, mob, cob, dog, fog, jog, log, hop, mop, top, nod, rod, pod

U: sun, bun, but, cut, hut, nut, bus, cup, pup, bug, dug, hug, jug, mug, rug, tug, bud, mud, cub, hub

LONG VOWELS IN CONSONANT-VOWEL-CONSONANT- E WORDS

A: face, lace, case, race, made, wade, cage, page, bake, cake, lake, make, rake, take, sale, tale, came, game, name, same, cane, mane, pane, cape, tape, base, case, vase, date, gate, late, cave, gave, save, wave, haze, maze

I: like, hike, pipe, ripe, wipe, bit, kite, five, dime, lime, time, file, mile, pile, tile, life, wife, hide, wide, mice, nice, rice

O: code, rode, robe, joke, woke, hole, pole, dome, home, bone, cone, lone, zone, note, hope, rope, hose, nose, rose, hole

U: tune, June, cube, tube, rule, mule, pure, sure

Selected Resources

Cressy, Judith. *What Can You Do with a Paper Bag?* San Francisco: Chronicle Books in association with The Metropolitan Museum of Art, 2001.

Dixon, Dougal and John Malam. *E.Guides: Dinosaur.* London: Dorling Kindersley Limited, 2004.

Driscoll, Michael, ill. Meredith Hamilton. *A Child's Introduction to Poetry.* New York: Black Dog and Leventhal Publishers, Inc., 2003.

Emberley, Ed. *Ed Emberley's Complete FunPrint Drawing Book.* New York: Little, Brown and Company, 2002.

Fry, Edward Bernard, Ph.D., Jacqueline E. Kress, Ed.D., and Dona Lee Fountoukidis. Ed.D. *The Reading Teacher's Book of Lists, Fourth Edition.* New Jersey: Prentice Hall, 2000.

Kohl, MaryAnn, ill. K. Whelan Dery. *Preschool Art: It's the Process, Not the Product.* Beltsville, Maryland: Gryphon House, 1994.

Mogilner, Alijandra. *Children's Writer's Word Book.* Cincinnati, Ohio: Writer's Digest Books, 1992.

Novelly, Maria C. *Theatre Games for Young Performers.* Colorado Springs, Colorado: Meriwether Publishing LTD, 1985.

Rosen, Michael, ed. *The Kingfisher Book of Children's Poetry.* New York: Kingfisher, 1993.

Wigg, Philip R. and Jean Hasselschwert. *A Handbook of Arts and Crafts, Tenth Edition.* New York: McGraw Hill, 2001.

Index

A
a 5, 9, 11-13, 16-18, 101-102, 105-107, 121-126
active rhymes 5-6, 10-11, 21-22, 35, 45, 48-49, 64, 71, 77-79, 81-82, 85-86, 92, 127-128
alphabet symbols 5-18, 21-31, 32, 40, 68-69
animals 5, 21,-22, 25, 39, 49, 53-56, 70, 96, 105-107
at home activities 15, 18, 24, 25, 28, 31, 36, 41, 66, 69, 88, 91, 110, 120, 123, 126

B
b 5, 9, 11-13, 16-18, 38-41, 103, 105-107, 114-116, 118
bats 39, 105-107
blue 60-62
bugs 21-22, 40-41, 85-86, 103-104, 118

C
c 5, 9, 11-13, 16-18
color 60-62, 108-110
comparison and contrast x, 10-11, 14, 74, 89-91, 105, 121, 131-132
complementary 60-62, 109-110
consonants 5-97, 101-104, 133, 135
crayons 7-10, 14, 17, 23, 30, 39, 46, 57, 61-62, 79, 84, 87, 91, 94, 106, 112, 116, 122, 131
creative thinking 7, 31, 37, 39, 46, 80, 87-88, 91, 97, 110, 116-117, 122, 132, 134
critical thinking x, 16, 19, 29, 32, 34-35, 42-43, 52, 55-56, 81, 111, 133

D
d 5, 9, 11-13, 16-18, 51-54, 95 (medial)
dinosaurs 53-54

E
e 5, 9, 11-13, 16-18, 108-110, 121-123

F
f 5, 9, 11-13, 15-18, 42-44
fish 112-113
flannel board patterns 17-18, 36, 70, 79, 85
form 45-46, 65-66, 68-69, 71-72, 87-88, 96, 103-104, 125-126

G
g 5, 9, 11-13, 15-18, 63-66, 95 (medial)
green 60-62, 78, 108

H
h 5, 9, 11-13, 14, 15-18, 32-33, 101, 131
hands 5, 32-33

I
i 6, 9, 11-13, 15-18, 45-47, 102, 111-113, 121-123, 127-130
imagination 7, 23, 27-28, 38-39

J
j 6, 9, 11-13, 15-18, 67-69
jewelry 7, 67-69

K
k 6, 9, 11-13, 15-18, 34-37, 129-130

L
l 6, 9, 11-13, 15-18, 45-47, 95 (medial)
letters 1-18, 21-32, 40, 68-69, 101-104, 133
line 33, 49-50, 83, 94, 132
long vowels 121-134
lower case 11, 14-15, 18

M
m 6, 9, 11-13, 15-18, 21-24, 95 (medial), 131-132
math 57-59, 75-76, 90, 119-120, 125-126
medial consonants 95-97, 136
mixing 61-62, 79-80
murals (and friezes) 30, 33, 90-91

N
n 6, 9, 11-13, 15-18, 48-50, 95-97 (medial), 101

O
o 6, 9, 11-13, 15-18, 102, 114, 121-123, 131-132
orange 60-62, 78
outdoor activities 17, 50

P
p 6, 9, 11-13, 15-18
paint 33, 61, 83, 94, 96, 109
paper plates 44
paper cutting 7-10, 30, 46-47, 75-76, 119-120, 124, 129, 130, 134
phonemes ix, xi, 5-97, 101-104, 133, 135, 99-136
phonics (definition) ix
picture books 2, 19-20, 90, 100, 125, 131, 134
prediction x, 51-52, 55-56, 95, 133
puppets 51-52, 119
purple 51-52, 60-62

Q
q 6, 9, 11-13, 89-91

R
r 6, 9, 11-13, 15-18, 70-73
rattle 71-72
red 60-62, 108

S
s 6, 9, 11-13, 15-18, 26-28
science 21-22, 26, 45, 49-50, 53-54, 61, 83, 108-113, 124
scissors 7-10, 8-9, 17-18, 23-25, 30-31, 39-40, 44, 46-47, 53-54, 57-59, 65-66, 75-76, 87, 96, 106, 112, 119-120, 125-126, 129-130
senses 49, 60, 64, 70, 85, 89, 113
sequence 5-18
short vowels 101-120
snakes 124
sounds 70-73, 85-86, 124
space 26, 45
staples 7, 46-47, 65, 68
surrealism 33
symbols 27-28, 33

T
t 6, 9, 11-13, 15-18, 29-31, 95 (medial), 101, 105-107
take-homes 15, 18, 24, 25, 28, 31, 36, 41, 66, 69, 88, 91, 97, 110, 120, 123, 126
time 83, 96 (seasons), 107 (time of day), 133 (month)
tracing 33, 50, 82
true or not true 29, 111

U
u 6, 9, 11-13, 15-18, 102-104, 118-123, 133-134
upper case 9, 84

V
v 6, 9, 11-13, 15-18, 77-80
vegetables 77-80
vowels 99-136

W
w 6, 9, 11-13, 15-18, 55-59
wax 92-94
weaving 57-59
web sites xii, 3, 20, 100, 125, 129, 134

X
x 6, 9, 11-13, 15-18, 92-94

Y
y 6, 9, 11-13, 15-18, 81-83
yellow 60-62, 82-83

Z
z 6, 9, 11-13, 15-18, 85-88
zigzag 76, 87-88

www.ingramcontent.com/pod-product-compliance
Lightning Source LLC
Chambersburg PA
CBHW081203240426
43669CB00039B/2795